I0528546

FINDING LOVE
AT 80

*The adventures of two very senior citizens
finding a new life together in a high tech world
as told by each partner*

by

Pris Keefer and Paul Mikos

FINDING LOVE AT 80

Copyright © 2023 by Pris Keefer and Paul Mikos
All rights reserved.

Published in the United States by
CLASS
Publishing Division
P.O. Box 2884
Pawleys Island, SC 29585
www.ClassAtPawleys.com

ISBN 978-1-955095-26-6

All photography restoration by Anne Swift Malarich.

Dedicated to
Each Other

Acknowledgments

We would like to thank Linda Ketron, our publisher who got excited enough about the concept to actually agree to publish our work, and for her guidance in how to do it. Also Mary Lou Cassingham for reading our first draft to see if the book had a chance to be published, or might be too boring. Carrie Humphreys for her initial support before anything was written and thought the concept was great.

Table of Contents

Introduction

We have written this book to help seniors who find themselves alone after a spouse's death or divorce. This is a tough period and can cause one to have some very unhealthy feelings. You can feel very lonely. Friends and family may be gone, and your previously familiar life may already have started to deteriorate. You may feel that you can go on with your life alone, or you may feel a strong desire for a new relationship.

What are the situations that an 80-year-old man and an 80-year-old woman face when they want to meet someone to share their lives with. We know, because we have experienced them first hand. From how to find a new partner, to internet dating, to actually meeting, and then... what happens if things seem to be working out? Do you live together? Do you get married? Do you move into your partner's house or buy a new home together? What is it like to meet your new partner's family and friends? If a major health crisis occurs, like Covid did in our case, how does it affect your new relationship?

Any 80-year-old is bound to be set in their ways. We felt that we didn't have time for a long courtship, and we didn't want to waste time determining our compatibility. We knew our cultural experiences could be completely different in the smallest ways, and they were. We would address differences in religious views, sexual activity, socializing, travel, entertainment, food, sports, life styles and lots more, as we lived our new lives together. There are two sides to everything, and they are not always the same for a man as they are for a woman.

Without reading each other's chapters until finished, we have written our own views of life together from January 2020, our first contact, until July of 2023, a little more than three years. In each chapter, Pris describes her view point of the topic, and then Paul tells his.

2

Prologue

We feel it would be very helpful that you understand what kind of life each of us had been living in recent history before our journey together began. So here we present a brief history of that period, unwashed, open, and truthful, down to the smallest detail.

PRIS

It was the fall of 1988. My husband of 27 years had just passed. We had had two children. My son was in his sophomore year of college and my daughter was happily married. She and her husband were trying to have a baby before my husband died but had not been successful. One day before he died she came to our house, went over to her father and said, "Dad, do not worry. God came to me last night and told me that I would have two boys." Two years after her father died, she had twin boys, her only children.

Six years later the school system where I was a teacher had a buyout opportunity. I could stay three more years in Cleveland, Ohio, or I could take the buyout of two years and retire with 29 years instead of the required 30 but get a little less money in my retirement. If I retired I would move to North Carolina where my daughter and her twin boys were living. Let's see… Cleveland, Ohio, for three more years with no family, or move now to North Carolina with my darling grandchildren. Well, that was a no-brainer! I sold my house myself and moved close to my daughter in North Carolina. Ten days after I moved there my daughter called me and said that her husband had been transferred to Chicago! I think I cried an ocean of tears.

Two years later I married husband number two. We moved to Myrtle Beach, SC, just a block from the ocean. I loved being near the beach but not so much my husband. Seven years later we were divorced.

I immediately found a house that was about to be built in Pawleys Island, SC. It was a spec house and the land had just been cleared. I was able to pick out all the colors, etc., which was really great. I bought it simply as a flip to sell in two years, so I had time to decide where I wanted to go. That was when my neighbor from Myrtle Beach found out that I was divorced and asked me to have dinner with him. He was also in the process of getting divorced. In South Carolina there is this antiquated law that says, unless there is proof of infidelity, there is a wait period of one whole year. That is ridiculous if no children are involved.

Two years later we were married at Pawleys Plantation where I lived. We enjoyed the good life of living in a country club atmosphere. We played golf with each other, as well as being in a league. We also had couples' bridge and went on cruises with both family and friends. Then one fateful day my husband decided to lift a heavy generator that he had just repaired from the trunk of his car. Alas! The generator started to fall and he tried to catch it. He broke his back and, even though he had surgery at the best spine clinic in Charleston, he never was without severe pain. For five years I nursed him in the best way I could. Meanwhile doctors kept giving him more opiates.

In November of 2018, he died in my arms. My little Havanese dog, Cody, and I mourned his death. My life became centered around Cody. He was cute, smart, and definitively the ruler of my home.

I decided that I needed to get away. I heard that some of the ladies in the Plantation were planning a trip to Italy. That was just what I needed! It was really a great trip. From Italy I went to Germany to reacquaint myself with a German friend who had lived with my family in 1957 as an AFS student. She and her husband took me 1st Class all over Germany, from train rides to front seats at plays, and to the best hotels. I loved it.

When I returned home I noticed that my little Cody was not acting right. I took him to the vet and he was diagnosed with cancer. I was told with a $5,000 operation he could live 3-6 months. I had the operation performed. He lasted three weeks! It seemed that everything I loved was gone. I could not go into a room without missing my Cody. Finally I went to visit my son who had just moved to the Kansas City, Kansas area. He has a little beagle who slept with me most nights. I stayed for a month. I hated to leave, but it was time for me to go home. My sorrow was not to end with Cody's dying. Shortly after, my mother, who was 99-1/2 years old, died unexpectedly. She was in a nursing home in Lenexa, Kansas. I could not get there in time before she died, but fortunately, my son was close by. He was with her when she took her last breath. For that I am grateful. It had been a disastrous year, and I was looking forward to 2020 to be a more positive experience.

The next chapter is what this book is all about. I wanted my readers to know a little bit about my life before the internet… before husband number four.

PAUL

Up until December 12, 2012, I was living a happy life with my wife, Bonnie. We had been married for 46 years, and on that day she died in her sleep without any warning. In fact, we had both just come back from an intense physical, passed by both of us with flying colors. It felt like I had lost my right arm.

I am going to tell you a little about myself before she died, so you can understand my mental state through the next few years. We had spent about 35 years or so living in Silicon Valley, California. In 1997 we moved to Paso Robles, C.A., and then, in 2007 we had moved from Paso Robles to Rock Hill, S.C., in order to take advantage of the lower state taxes and generally lower living expenses. In the ten years we lived in Paso Robles and before Bonnie died, our son (Brian) visited us once, and our daughter (Pam) never visited at all.

In the 46 years of our married life, we raised two children, a boy and his older sister. My son was a quiet guy who did various sports and was an average student in school. Except for a little under-age beer drinking, he mostly stayed out of trouble. He started playing soccer at a very early age, and I volunteered to coach his teams. This got me interested in the sport, and I started playing in an adult league. One of the highlights of my relationship with him was when he joined the same league and we played together on the same team. He was in his 20s and I was in my mid-40s. I really enjoyed that period, and we continued to play regularly on Sunday mornings until he went off to college. When he was growing up, we did many sports together, including snow skiing, racketball, camping, and small plane flying trips. We enrolled him in a summer crash course to improve his self-esteem and grades when he was in high school, so he could get into college. He graduated from college, got a teacher's credential and now teaches in Oregon. While in college, he came home regularly, ate with us, did his laundry and appeared to be a typical college student. We visited him often and always seemed to have a good time.

Brian and Pam, my daughter, came to South Carolina for their mother's funeral and stayed one day. About a month after the funeral, I flew out to Redding, C.A., where Brian was currently living. We went out to dinner after work in the evening and then took a drive to San Jose, C.A., on the weekend and visited my daughter Pamela. We went out to dinner and stayed in a motel. We didn't get an invitation to stay in her three-bedroom home. We had breakfast at Pam's home and then hopped back in the car and drove back to Northern California, about six hours each way. During this trip everything seemed to be pleasant, and we had what appeared to me to be a good time.

A couple of weeks later I called Brian just to say hello, and he told me his "shrink" said that he should not talk to me for awhile. I tried to find out what the problem was and he would not discuss it. That was the last time I talked to him. Letters and e-mails continue to go unanswered. He is not married to the best of my knowledge.

My daughter Pamela, on the other hand, was always in trouble. She seemed to carry a lot of anger which started when she was four or five. When she started school, she didn't do her schoolwork and cut classes, fought constantly with her parents and teachers, and had few friends.

The incident that stands out to this day is her first social event as she was just starting high school. It was a social for incoming students, and I drove her to the school. I set a place for us to meet in the parking lot when the dance was over. Well, I showed up at the appointed time and place and waited as the kids came pouring out of the dance. I waited and waited, but there was no Pamela. As the crowd disappeared, I was starting to get worried. When there was no one left, I was about to go inside to see where she was. At that very moment a policeman came to my car window and asked me my name. When I told him, he informed me that Pam was being held under arrest for getting in a fist fight with the principal of the school while being heavily intoxicated. This was a continuation of her problems with alcohol and drugs. Her future was to be filled with troubles, quitting high school without really getting started and disappearing for days at a time from our home.

We spent a small fortune on counseling with sessions for the three of us together, a second one with Pam by herself, and a third one with Bonnie and me by ourselves, three sessions every week. During this time, Pam moved in with a boy when she was about fourteen, and they eventually got married. They still live in San Jose, California. Pam's husband had his tubes tied early in their relationship, so there are no grandchildren involved at all. At Bonnie's funeral she was pleasant, but only stayed one night. The last time I saw her was shortly after the funeral when Brian and I drove to San Jose. She will not take my calls.

In 2007, Bonnie and I decided to travel around the country in our 36-foot RV. We had already made two trips across the country with no goal except to visit the country and sightsee. By this time we had sold our California home and decided to stop when we found a place we liked. We saw the handwriting on the wall with the problems of California living and decided to get out before we couldn't. We ended up in South Carolina.

We enjoyed our lives a great deal, we traveled a lot and generally enjoyed ourselves. We had very few friends in our new city. My wife's sister and niece whom we were very close to had both died recently. My children were both on the West Coast and I gave up trying to make contact with them. As my wife and I did everything together, I was very alone when she passed. After she died, I spent the next nine years in a state of emptiness.

The above is my family situation as I write this in July 2023.

Little did I know how things were going to change in the near future.

Chapter 1

GETTING ON THE INTERNET

PRIS

My daughter decided that I needed to go on the internet. I am not sure what her reason was for thinking so. It was too early after my husband's death; I was not ready. In November I decided to try it. She had set me up on Senior Match. So I decided to go on the internet, but I had some questions I had to ask myself. Why was I even looking on the internet for someone? Who was I looking for? Was I looking for companionship or secretly in my mind was I looking for a permanent partner? I decided it was for companionship. After all, what man would want a wrinkled old body and sagging boobs in an 81-year-old.

I realized right away that there were some things I needed to know about online dating. First, a wink meant that you wanted to have a conversation with that person. If they found your profile interesting, they would wink back. Second, I learned that people lie about their age. I put down my real age and got only one response. After all, who would want to date an 81-year-old! The first response online was a disaster. If you asked a senior citizen what "catfished" meant, you probably would be met with a perplexed expression. But if you used the word "catfished" to someone under 50, they would know immediately. It is just another one of those generation gaps.

A man winked at me on the Senior Match website. Yay! A response! This person was very nice looking in his picture and knew all the right things to say to a lonely 81-year-old lady. I was having fun; I have to admit, but something did not seem right. I needed to find out if this person was legitimate. I found that there are places on the internet that you can go and find out information about people. I looked up the address where he said that he lived. It did not really surprise me that the couple who owned and lived in the house did not have the same last name as his. He also only contacted me late in the evening. If you think about it, there is about a six hour difference in time, if he was contacting me from the Ukraine. As an engineer, he said he had to go to the Ukraine on business. This was obviously before the war in Ukraine. And lo and behold, when he got there, he claimed that he had been robbed and beaten, and could I please send him some money. "Sure," I said. "Do you want $10K or $20K?" "Oh," he replied, "$20K would be fine." At that point my Christian upbringing went right out the window with my reply. So that is what it means to be "catfished." And men, do not think it can't happen to you. I found his picture under different names so I contacted Senior Match. I also notified the other women with whom he was talking and warned them. This unfortunately did not deter him. He kept texting me and telling me he could not believe I would be so mean to him! Finally, I am guessing that Senior Match shut him down because I no longer heard from him. I cannot begin to tell you how empty this whole experience left me. I had to remember that I was not the bad person here.

There is another website called Christian Mingle. On that online dating site you are required to set up a profile of yourself and then they match you with people who have the same likes and dislikes as you do. If I had used this website, I would never have met Paul because we are totally different in many ways, and it is working just fine!

The night of January 6, 2020, I checked the Senior Match website. I was somewhat skeptical after being "catfished" but I decided to try it again. I was certainly going to be more careful this time and for sure watch out for those sweet talkers. What was I looking for? I was not interested particularly in a fourth marriage or even living with someone. I wanted someone to open doors for me, have great conversations, and perhaps someone to travel with. This particular night there was a gentleman from Rock Hill which was close to Charlotte where my daughter lived. It would be nice to meet someone who lived close to her, so that I could go out to dinner or just be friends in general. So I sent this Rock Hill person a WINK. I checked the senior site several times to see if there was any response to my wink… nothing! The next morning I checked again… nothing! Finally that evening there was a response. The first thing that he told me was that he was not 76 but would soon be 81. He explained that he did this because he did not think anyone would wink at him if he said that he was in his 80's. I had begun to think the same thing. Both of us, it seemed, had given up ever meeting someone to possibly spend the rest of our lives with. Much later he told me that the reason he responded to my wink was my smile and my profile, which not only said very little but also gave no restrictions, such as a possible companion had to go to church every Sunday, or could not smoke, or must love old movies.

After communicating online by typing messages for several days, we started calling each other at least once every day, but most of the time twice a day. Our conversations would last anywhere from one to two hours. He had led a very interesting and adventurous life, and I loved listening to his stories. Through our conversations we learned a lot about each other. Never in his emails nor in our phone conversations with each other did he step over the line, and there was never mention of anything sexual or sensuous. We just had great conversations and got to know each other. Also, never once during this time did we use the Facetime option. We both agreed that we would rather wait to meet each other face to face. I believe that getting to know each other by phone and texting before we actually met was the key to our relationship today.

Meeting someone for an hour over a cup of coffee does not expose the true character of a person. Living four hours apart, our options for meeting were limited. He suggested that we meet in Florence, South Carolina for a cup of coffee, since that is halfway for us both. My response to that was, "I will not drive four hours for just a cup of coffee." It was later that I realized how that sounded. I suggested that he and his dog would come to my house at Pawleys Island and stay in a motel nearby. However, it turned out that the week we chose was a holiday weekend and the nearest motel with a vacancy that accepted dogs was 35 miles away. Finally, we decided that when I would go to Charlotte to see my daughter, I would stop by his house in Rock Hill and he would fix me lunch.

Earlier I mentioned going to a website that lets you research a person and you can learn many details about the person you're researching. They usually charge a small fee for the first few days and then after that the price will increase. After being catfished, I used that service for information on my Rock Hill friend, Paul. I verified that everything he had told me was fact. However, he failed to tell me about his ticket for driving without his seat belt. LOL (laughing out loud)

PAUL

I thought I could live out my life alone and made a good effort to do so, but the loneliness just kept on building until I started to wonder why I was still hanging around. I had a dog. She was my main companion, and I loved her dearly. She just was not a good conversationalist.

I had hobbies, I was a pilot and had built my own bi-plane. I spent a lot of time at the airport. I fussed at little odds and ends on the plane to keep busy, and made friends with a few of the other pilots. But generally, they were only casual acquaintances. Most of the other pilots weren't around as often as I was because of jobs, etc. I played poker often at night. I had played for years and was serious about the game, but now I found myself going more for company than to improve my skills. Many times I went on trips with groups of other players, primarily to Florida to play in big tournaments. Needless to say, I was much older than most of the folks I played with, so we had a major gap in life histories and interests. We did have fun, but I always felt a little like an outsider to the youthful group. These hobbies kept me entertained socially, but I always came home to an empty house. The dog and my hobbies only went so far, and I started to wonder if my life was going to stay so empty.

Getting Myself onto the Internet

Eventually I found out about "Senior Match Up" and looked into it. I was in my early 70s and didn't expect to find too many women interested in meeting an old guy with a giant bald spot on the back of his head, one new knee, two new hips, and who talked with a Brooklyn accent (where I grew up and had never lost the accent).

Bonnie was religious (Catholic), and was finishing her BS degree and actually had enough credits to get a degree when she died. She was very smart and could speak four languages. She managed our bank accounts and kept the bills paid. She was generally well aware of world politics and planned all our travels; plus, I had spent 46 years eating her fine cooking. We traveled together both on business and pleasure, which made us somewhat worldly in our outlooks. It was going to be hard to find someone in Rock Hill, to match her talents.

I did make some decisions about who I was going to be looking for. Age was the big criteria for me. Most of my poker buddies were under 40, and all they could think about for me was having a 30-year-old trophy woman to hang on my arm and having great sex with a real Miss Hottie. At my age that was like a 30-year-old guy going out with a 12-year-old – not too much in common. I wanted someone that I could talk to and share new life experiences with. I wanted someone who still liked sex (but not too often) and could and would cook more than eat out every night. I cooked myself and liked to experiment with new dishes, especially international cuisine. I also wanted someone that traveled at least a little. There were many ladies in the area that had not ever been out of the county they lived in. I wanted someone who dressed well and would be comfortable in any environment.

This may sound like a lot to ask, and it was.

The Faux Pas King Speaks
So I sat down and wrote a short biography and a description of what I thought I was looking for. This is where my Californian culture mind had a little trouble thinking as a South

Carolinian. I made some pretty good faux pas. For example: you don't tell an older South Carolinian woman that you're not religious. This is the Bible Belt! Next, you can't mention that you actually gamble for money; completely illegal down here, both law-wise and Baptist-wise.

Now, there is a characteristic about the people I noticed very soon upon my arrival in the south. I didn't expect to meet a Marilyn Monroe look-alike down here, and I didn't have any preconceived notions about looks. They are not all that important to me. But there was one characteristic that I knew I didn't want. It was an OBESE woman! So I made a note of it in my wish list.

The biggest faux pas ever. I got buckets full of emails for weeks saying how insensitive I was. But I already knew that. Thank You.

Of course my comment had to go, and it went.

So I had to use my powers of observation to determine if I was getting what I wasn't looking for, their picture. This led me to another little quirk that one must be aware of. Pictures tell a thousand words about a person, all except when they were taken. I never saw so many 70-year-olds that looked like they were 35. It meant that I had to meet them to see who they really were.

Online It Is

And so I went online, waiting anxiously to see who the computer thought was correct for me. Actually the computer doesn't do anything but give you access to communicate with all the ladies that are looking for a man on their website. You have to go through them and decide which ones may be of interest to you. Of course you are now posted on the site and the women out there are doing the same inspection of you.

When you find someone you think is a fit, you send them a "wink" which alerts them to your interest. If they want to communicate further, they will contact you for further analysis.

One of my prerequisites was that they lived within a few hours drive before I would consider a meeting. This requisite had to eventually change and periodically I had to extend my search farther and farther. I would like to point out here that I am not big on driving long distances, but by golly! I ended up driving four hours each way to visit my new honey's home.

The Winks Start Coming In

I didn't have high hopes but I started getting winks. I was surprised at the number, but volume does not equal quality. I got about a dozen replies quickly and started to communicate with them. I tried to ask some questions in our initial contacts and be as subtle as possible about details that interested me. I was further surprised to see the quality of the pictures that were posted. There were several clear-cut types.

The first type were pictures taken during family outings and other natural events. They didn't look posed or staged. It was possible to tell what kind of life the person led recently. For example, if the lady's picture showed her in a bar and obviously intoxicated, with a man or two hanging onto her, she probably wasn't going to be someone I would want to spend a lot of time with. The majority in this category were pictures showing the ladies at picnics, parties or sporting events with lots of friends around them. They would appear to be having fun.

The second type was ladies who had paid for a portfolio of

staged pictures. They would be taken in perfect locations without any friends or activities that she may have been a part of. She would be dressed perfectly for the staged background in the picture under ideal conditions. This showed me someone that didn't do things with friends or relatives, or she might even be desperate.

The third class of photo was someone who looked like she was wearing an old homemade house dress, with no hairstyling, standing by herself in front of a church or in the kitchen, looking very somber. She didn't look like someone I could travel with outside of Rock Hill.

Of course there were exceptions. There was one lady that had all her pictures taken in a negligee. She appeared to be about 50 years old. They were taken in various sultry poses and definitely conveyed to me that she was looking for an old guy who would leave her his estate without having to wait too long.

Another major thing I noticed was that most winks were coming from outside of the Rock Hill area. So I picked the closest ones that sounded interesting and made some dates. The routine was to meet at a convenient Starbucks about 10 a.m. and try hard to remember what their picture was like, so it was possible to find them. I always offered to buy a coffee for the lady. But surprisingly many of them insisted on buying their own . (Oh Oh – maybe she could be a radical women's libber here). So we would chat about mundane things and try to get a feel for who we were.

Many of the women had absolute ideas about what they wanted and put them in their write-ups. For example –

- You must go to their church.
- You must play bridge, or worse, if you want to get together with me, you cannot disturb my current bridge schedule for any reason.

- If we get together, you must allow my adult child to live with us.
- She has three large dogs that need a lot of space and medical treatments.
- She will not cook or clean house.
- She wants us to go to church all the time.
- She hasn't had sex in years and that's fine with her.
- She will not leave the neighborhood that she lives in now.

But the winner was "You must want to host dinner parties every weekend with 10 or 12 couples who are your closest friends." I couldn't achieve that, even today.

These are actual statements that were in many wish lists. Did these women think that there was such a high demand for someone that they could pre-cancel winks based on narrow criteria? There is no reason for you to be surprised by what some of the ladies want. Remember, as you read this, it's not your fault; these are part of their original write-ups. They want you to fit in with their lifestyle, and let's not worry about what you want. Needless to say, I passed over these folks because I definitely didn't want a person with rigid ideas. I'm too old to bend around somebody else's plans for me. So here is a short description of what some of them appeared to be like after the initial meeting. Some of these were of interest to me because I couldn't believe what they had written and I had to meet them and see if they were really serious. I had nothing else to do and I wanted to give anyone a chance that might be a fit for me, or actually see if they were really as weird as their write-ups portrayed them to be. It became a form of entertainment for me, as I didn't have much to do anyway.

At this juncture, I would like to point out an old expression written by a very wise old man:

"YOU HAVE TO KISS A LOT OF FROGS BEFORE YOU FIND A PRINCE(SS)."

A Long-term, Long-distance Relationship
I only had one long-distance communication that I thought sounded interesting. Normally, I either decided right away to meet the ladies or not meet them at all. We had several long texts back and forth and then started talking on the phone. She lived in the suburbs of Providence, Rhode Island, so this was quite a distance from where I lived, and she was still working. She eventually started suggesting that we meet in Providence, and I was considering it. She sounded very provocative and sensuous and seemed to be really interested in me herself. After awhile, I asked her how many guys had come to Providence to see her and, after thinking for awhile, she said four. I then asked her if she had any interest in the men she had met. She said, "No, they just went sightseeing and had dinner for three or four days and then they went home." I said that I didn't want to travel so far for a dinner date, and had no interest in sightseeing in Providence. I never did quite understand what she had in mind, but it definitely was not a long-term relationship.

So It's Off to Starbucks I Will Go, Hi Ho, Hi Ho
Now let me tell you about some of the ladies I actually met for coffee. I include these so you can see the wide variety of persons that you can come across. I can't remember all of them or what order they appeared in, but their stories are real.

A woman who, upon meeting in a Starbucks, suggested we play some games – this was immediately after saying "hello." My favorite thing not to do is play games with a total stranger anywhere, let alone in a public place. She was very insistent, so

I finally agreed and after a short while I remembered another appointment far away and left.

Then there was a woman that wanted to meet at a doggy park, which sounded OK. We went to a nice park she knew and strolled and talked. Our dogs strolled along and seemed to like each other. She was very concerned about her dog, a full-size German Shepherd which had broken its back and was going through rehabilitation. She also had to get out of her apartment and was looking for a new place to live (presumably with me). She also had an adult son who was "temporarily" out of work and living with her. One date only, thank you.

There was a lady who gave ghost tours, wrote ghost hunting books and was very serious about ghosts. As I have a heavy scientific background, it was very hard for me not to laugh. My only reaction was my inquisitiveness at how she could make a living chasing ghosts. Her entire ghost interest didn't come out until we actually met.

Then there was a lady that was a junior college teacher who wanted to meet at the Cracker Barrel after work. When she came into the restaurant, she was dressed like a 1960s hippie girl. I couldn't believe it. She was a little older than me, but that was not the problem. She wanted to teach until she died which was okay, too, but she made nearly nothing and lived from hand to mouth. She also mentioned her politics a little. They were different than mine by a whole lot. She was a very nice person and I really liked her, but we could never make a life together, because I came from an intense business and scientific background, and she was a flower child who never got over it.

Another one I met made a very positive impression on me at first. She was a lady that had a small condominium not far from where I lived. We hit it off pretty well. The problem with her, which wouldn't be a problem for many guys, was that she didn't drive. She had an accident recently, and she had developed a total fear of driving. She took Uber everywhere she went. So, after our meeting, I drove her home and she invited me in to see her condo. It was a very small one-bedroom unit, and I thought it was a bad idea for her to let me in; after all, I could have been Jack the Ripper. I didn't call her again, because I saw myself becoming her chauffeur, and I thought she didn't have much good sense.

Then there was a lady I called China Doll. She was of Chinese descent (not a problem) and had a wholesale business which took her to China often. She expected me to travel with her, but this did not interest me, as I had been to China many times already and had no interest in commuting back and forth. She also had a hard driving personality and was very demanding for a first date.... I was looking to mellow out – no sale!

Another lady had a sister who was very ill, and she needed to take care of her sister nearly full time. She looked very worn out and tired for her age when we met. She thought her sister was getting well enough, so that she could finally have a little life of her own. So we went out to dinner a few times, and she finally said she couldn't keep up with juggling two separate lives. She felt guilty every time she left her sister alone. She broke it off with me. I was sorry because we had a lot in common.

There was a lady who lived a short distance from where I lived. She appeared to be compatible with me; until she mentioned politics and she proved to be 180 degrees out of phase with me and was very vocal about her views. She was a political junky. Me, not at all. Sorry, no deal.

One lady I met for coffee on a Sunday morning sounded like

22

she might work out. She even grew up in Brooklyn, as I did. So off to Starbucks I went. She was waiting for me in her car and when she got out, there to my distress she was – Miss Obese. I was pretty shocked to see her, but I wanted to be a gentleman and we walked over to Starbucks and sat outside and had our coffees and a very long talk. We really hit it off, and I even asked her to brunch at a restaurant in the same mall. We probably spent about four hours together before we left. I backed away from her future phone calls after I decided that I would not feel good about her looks over the long term. I was really sorry because she and I really were compatible and got along the best of all those I had met to date. I just couldn't see myself in bed with her.

If this sounds like I was being overly critical about the people I was meeting, it was because most of them didn't mention their idiosyncrasies, which I later found out about during our meetups. Another side to this search was that, even though several of these women did seem like normal persons, there didn't seem to be any magnetism or connection of any kind between us. Remember that I was very lonely and willing to give anyone a chance to have a relationship possibly work out after getting to know them. I had nothing to do all day but look and I really wanted to find a partner.

Finally, I met a lady that seemed like we could have a conversation. Her picture showed her in a business suit with her blonde hair pulled back in a tight professional-looking style. She was about the same age as myself. We seemed to hit it off quite well and had several dates. She had been a real estate agent and entrepreneur.

One night while having dinner at a local restaurant, I told

her I was scheduled to have knee surgery, but would be alone during the recovery. She immediately offered to let me use her basement apartment in her home, which I gladly accepted. I was rather surprised because we did not know each other very well and had not been intimate yet. But she lived up to her commitment, and I stayed in her basement apartment for about two months. I started staying at my home during the week after my recovery and going to her place on weekends.

She was very wealthy and lived in a very large house right on a lake with no close neighbors. She spent all her time in her gardens and was very tired every night, including the weekends I came to visit. We would eat dinner, and she would fall asleep in her chair almost immediately. My life came down to helping her in the garden all weekend, with the same routine each night. On occasion we went out to eat in a small restaurant which I didn't like much because it only served fried foods. But it was the only game in town.

We went on like this for a couple of years, but I never could get serious about my feelings for her, so we slowly drifted apart. After the breakup, I didn't look at the internet website for many months, and I started spending a lot of time watching old movies on TV all day. I was starting to draw the conclusion that meeting someone online was not going to work for me, and I was not going to renew my membership in Senior Match Up.

But... during this time my name had stayed active on the senior match list, so I started doing the coffee circuit again. My subscription was about to run out and after several more attempts at trying to find a compatible person, I again gave up and decided not to renew it. I also felt that, if I had a hard time meeting someone when I was 72, now that I was 80, it would be a miracle to find someone.

Pris and I Meet Online

Then, on the last day of my subscription, I received an email from a lady named Pricilla. Instead of the short "canned" notice that usually started communications, she wrote a very long letter telling me about her life in the past year and accentuated her current state of loneliness. This was very different from the usual introductory contact, and I attributed it to the very long description I had put on senior match recently. After my last relationship, I had decided to really open up and "bare my soul" in my internet description. I read her page of details and the big thing that struck me as unusual was it didn't specify any details at all. She didn't fill out any of the canned responses. I liked this because defining absolutes without knowing the person may cause you to ignore a perfect match, except for one of these less than critical characteristics she might list. So normally, I wouldn't contact anyone who introduced themselves without writing anything. She had no statement of any kind written about herself. Despite my decision to stop trying to meet someone through Senior Match, I thought I would make one more attempt at getting acquainted. I wrote her back and eventually suggested we go to phone calls instead of writing back and forth. So we did.

Her description on the internet was very brief. She wrote that she was 81 and would know the right guy when she saw him. That's it. Now that's really something, even though I lied about my age and had listed my age as 76. I didn't think that anyone would be interested in someone 80 or more (like me).

We started talking every night for several hours, and I found that she was a very interesting person and we had a lot to share. We did not use Facetime because we didn't want our first visual exposure to be a less than perfect video image of either of us.

We agreed that we would wait for a live meeting. We had to meet eventually, and I suggested that we meet for coffee halfway between our cities. Her response threw me for a loop as she said that she would not drive for two hours for a cup of coffee and that she would come up to my city to meet. Wow! I was starting to think that there may be something wrong with her to be that aggressive. Actually her aggressiveness did not scare me. So I said if she was going to drive all the way to my city, then I would make us a lunch at my home. I hoped this would appear to be a very relaxed setting and she agreed.

The outcome of our first date contained more than one surprise ...

Chapter 2
THE FIRST DATE

PRIS

What was I thinking? After all, I am a retired teacher with a MA degree... educated. So what happened to my cognitive thinking skills? My friends warned me. My daughter begged me not to do it. Oh yes, I had been told by well-meaning friends, "Keep the motor running" and "Look for freshly dug mounds in the back yard." Yet here I was, pulling up into a stranger's driveway.

Paul met me halfway down the sidewalk to his front door. We greeted with a hello embrace. Later he told me that I was shaking quite a bit, which I do not doubt. He poured me a glass of wine and then served us a little appetizer, which neither of us can remember what it was. Like all first dates we talked a lot about ourselves and our previous lives. We sat on the sofa and listened to an Elvis Presley disk of gospel music.

Later he fixed Ma Poa Bean Curd. It was rather spicy and was made with tofu which I had never tasted before, and I can't say that I have since become a fan of it. But every now and then I appease his taste buds by agreeing to his fixing us the Ma Poa Bean Curd. We had a very pleasant afternoon. I think because of our three weeks of talking on the phone about three hours a day, we felt very comfortable with each other.

27

As I was preparing to leave around 5 o'clock the skies had become filled with dark clouds and night was falling. The trip to my daughter's was 35 minutes away. As I was getting into my car, the phone rang. It was my daughter. "Mom, if you feel at all comfortable, stay there for the night as it is sleeting here and I feel it would be too dangerous for you to drive here." Now Paul had already offered to sleep on the sofa if I wanted to stay and of course I declined. But now it seemed I had no choice. I stayed two more nights and Paul was the perfect gentleman. It was at this point I believe that I was, as my grandmother use to say, "smitten."

On my way back to the beach I stopped again to spend two more days getting to know Paul a little better. As I took my things to his bedroom, he commented, "I don't think I will be sleeping on the sofa tonight." And I just smiled.

PAUL

It was late January, 2020, and I was now 81.

I heard the car come up the driveway. For the past three or four years, no one came up the driveway except The Church of the Latter Day Saints recruiters or pizza delivery cars. It wasn't a surprise to hear it, because we had been talking on the phone for several weeks. Two or three hours at a time about nothing in particular, but always interesting and relaxing. We had made a plan to meet today.

She drove to my house from a beach town (Pawleys Island) three and a half hours away. I had offered to drive halfway to her place, for lunch or coffee, but she rejected that idea and said she would drive here, and now she was here. Fear and trepidation filled me more than I could remember ever in the past. This was it, after eight years of being alone. I was determined to do my very best to present myself in a way that would not scare her off. I heard the car door open and close. The dog started barking and I knew it was time to open the front door. I wanted to greet her without waiting for the bell to ring. My anxiety level increased, and I felt even more fear than I had known for a long time as I opened the door. What would her first reaction be to me? How would she be dressed? Would she look like her picture or would she be heavier or older looking? Would she have a personality and style about her that I would want to be around on a daily basis? I knew she had a Masters Degree, but not what she had done for a living.

As I opened the door carefully so that the dog stayed inside, I saw her at the bottom of the steps. A big smile crossed her face and her dimples accentuated her smiling eyes. She was petite, dressed modern, and carried herself like a lady as she walked towards me. I relaxed and gave her my best greeting hug with what I hoped was a smiling, comforting facial expression.

I said, "Glad to meet you, Pricilla." She gave me a warm look and returned my smile. So now she was on my doorstep and her smile melted me immediately. She came inside and she played with my dog a little while I hung up her coat.

I had pre-prepared a Chinese lunch with some fancy hors d'oeuvres. I thought I would impress her with one of my favorite dishes, Ma Pao Bean Curd. She seemed to enjoy it, even though it was slightly spicy and made with bean curd, an ingredient she had never tasted before. I had a slight feeling that I should have made something a little less exotic and started to get nervous about how she felt about the food. She insisted she really liked it and this was a new experience for her.

Her manner was very relaxed and at ease as we talked about her drive north and the warnings she got from relatives and friends about coming to my home for this first meeting. Some things were truly funny and bordered on the ridiculous. "Keep the car engine running during the initial meeting," "Don't go inside under any circumstances," "Look for fresh mounds of digging in the back yard," "Stay on the phone the whole time you're there," and on and on. She laughed at them and said at 81, she wasn't worried about much of anything.

From her online introduction, there were no demands that the person she was looking for like certain foods, belong to a certain church, do specific activities, or be of a certain type in any way. This struck me as highly unusual. I had stopped paying for my membership in the dating service because I didn't have any luck with the people I had met so far. There were many weirdoes, demanding or controlling types, and women that lived very far away. I had given up!

As we become senior citizens, it is my belief that you become more tolerant of opposing views, different lifestyles, and ideas for the future. Why do I feel this way? I am a conservative Republican from New York City, have an engineering degree, and have spent my work life in the high stress technical environment of Silicon Valley, California. I have traveled the world on business and pleasure, been very active in sports as a player and not a watcher, and I don't shy away from risk taking in my business or financial life. I was married to one women for 46 years, with no serious bumps along the way.

Pricilla is a liberal Democrat who grew up in the north and southern Midwest, has a teaching credential, and spent her career as a teacher at the middle school level of public schools. She has been married three times, had one divorce and two deaths in her married life. She doesn't like physical sports or work, anything done at higher elevations, and is very conservative financially. She is seriously religious and goes to church regularly. She hasn't eaten much of anything outside of the standard franchise or basic southern type food, but so far she has been willing to explore new things with me.

She spent that first night in my bed while I slept on the couch. In the morning she continued her trip north to visit her daughter. This gave me a chance to think about everything that occurred in our first meeting, the dinner, and my initial reaction to her.

Second Visit

A few days later, on her way home from visiting her daughter, she came back to my home and spent a few days. I initially stayed on the coach and she in my bed for the first couple of nights. This was a very anxious time for me, as I had had cancer of the prostate several years back and the doctor told me my chances of having sex were very small. I did explain during our phone conversations that I had had a new experimental treatment that gave me better odds of being able to perform. She said don't worry, it won't be the end of the world without any sexual activity.

As we talked that evening, I sensed that she wanted us to make an attempt at getting intimate, and I suggested that we share my bed. So with great apprehension I joined her in some tentative cuddling and gradually into heavy lovemaking. I couldn't believe that this was happening to me, and I was completely able to perform. At 81 she acted like a 20-year-old and we had an unbelievable time! I knew my doctor didn't take into consideration that I would meet someone like Pricilla.

31

The morning led to much discussion about her feelings for me and mine for her. We knew that this was the start of something big. The magnetism was definitely there. I couldn't walk past her without a big hug and a bigger kiss. She was a very warm and cuddly person that made me want to be with her every minute. Already I had strong feelings for her and didn't want her to leave.

At one point in our conversation, she left the living room and disappeared for short time. When she came back, she was wearing her coat and I thought something was the matter. I thought she was going to leave. Did I do something wrong? Did I hurt her feelings somehow? I stood up and walked towards her. When I got close, she dropped her coat onto the floor and there she stood, stark naked. She said to me "What you see is what you get." And laughed sensuously. I was totally relieved and surprised to see her like this. I let out a big laugh and pulled her towards me and gave her a big kiss. I was very excited about this and off we went into the bedroom where I proceeded to show her that I heartily approved. She wanted me to see her in broad daylight so that I would know what an 80-year-old women looked like in the raw. No makeup, or soft lighting, just out in the open. I was actually surprised to see that her body was in very fine shape and not what you would expect. I was pleased and exceedingly happy. This lady had everything a man could want.

After spending a few days together, she went home and I thought and thought about our meeting and I couldn't wait to see her again. I had just spent eight years of being alone, and I was on the edge of giving up hope of having any kind of life. I was about as low as you could get and still get up in the morning. Things were looking up. She told me early on that she didn't watch much TV. This was hard to believe. My days were spent watching news shows and old movies. I had nothing to do every day. Didn't play golf, fish, or other time-passing senior activities. But now, we sit for hours with some soft music playing in the background and have long conversations on many subjects. We both like to experiment with each other's meals and cooking styles.

The first date was over and it lasted a week. I knew my life was about to change for the better.

January 22, 2020 ~ The week we met.

Chapter 3

GETTING TO KNOW EACH OTHER

PRIS

It was dark and pouring down rain when Paul finally arrived at my door. When he arrived he exclaimed, "There will never be another four days that we are apart!" He was, of course, referring to the four days since I left his house. I felt the same way. It was a great week. I think I was falling in love. I was tingling all over.

Differences in Lifestyles

The contrast of where we lived and our houses was phenomenal. He lived in the country. When you pass a house with a tire swinging from a tree, you know that you are in the country. Of course, the cows and horses that you passed on the way to his house was another sure sign. In contrast, my house was on Pawleys Island in a gated Jack Nicklaus golf course community with houses that had manicured lawns.

But none of that mattered as the times we spent at each other's houses were nothing but memorable.

The Low Country

We took a trip to Brookgreen Gardens where he posed for a picture of his leg in an alligator's mouth. Not to fear, the alligator was only one of many sculptures at the garden. Brookgreen

34

Gardens is a 9,000+ acre private property which preserves the historic site's natural and cultivated landscape. People also come to this beautiful garden to see the display of spectacular sculptures. It was February so we missed the beauty of the azaleas and other flowers, but we did get to enjoy the sculptures. We also got to celebrate the otters' birthday. We enjoyed cake provided by the Gardens while the otters enjoyed a fish dinner. It was Paul's first encounter with multiple alligators. Not a favorite meeting.

A Taste of the South

South Carolina is famous for its barbeque. And luck had it that there was such a cook-off in Pawleys Island that weekend complete with bagpipes. Oops! Bagpipes are not Southern for sure, but everyone, including Paul, enjoyed them. For non-Southerners, a cook-off is where multiple chefs from the area compete for the prize of being the #1 barbeque chef in the area. All of the crowd gets to vote. It was held in a mini-mall with about 40 or 50 entries, and they all were very good. The turnout of folks supporting the event was amazing. It was a fun-filled day that we would do again in a minute.

Golf

Another unforgettable experience was our outing on the golf course. The Grand Strand, which includes 60 miles on the coast of the Carolinas, is famous for its golf courses. So it was only natural that I should suggest that we play a round of golf. Paul is not a golfer, which did not take me long to realize. I had received a box of golf balls for Christmas. The back nine on Pawleys Plantation golf course is located on a marsh, so while playing two of the holes, one must hit the ball over the marsh. There are also several ponds. Of course, Paul did not make it over any of them. "I can get over. Just give me one more ball. Just give me one more ball. Just give me one more ball." Needless to say, my Christmas gift was more than slightly depleted. For you golfers, it was a slow day at the golf course, so we did not hold anyone up. Again, Paul had the pleasure of meeting some of Pawleys Plantation's illustrious residents... alligators. A common sight all through the golf course is the abundance of alligators that are everywhere. He was intrigued, but also a little apprehensive.

The Beach

Of course, a trip to Pawleys Island would not be complete without a trip to the beach. He wanted to go surfing. So we bought two paddle boards and headed for the beach. Now keep in mind that we are talking about two 80-plus-year-olds, one of whom cannot swim. So we hit a couple of gentle waves and all went well. And then! The big mama wave came in and we both took quite a ride in the sand as the wave violently washed us ashore. Several people rushed to us to make sure we were all right including a very voluptuous young lady to help Paul. What fun! But that was our last attempt at surfing. As we were preparing to pack up our things and leave, a young man come over to us and said, "I hope that when my wife and I are your age, we can be as happy as you two are." And readers, that has not changed.

No Longer White-headed

In February, Covid had not really started in full force. People were still eating out. Valentine's Day was approaching. I diverge to the past here to tell you that around the age of 60, I decided that dying my hair brown every few weeks was too expensive so I thought about becoming a blonde, which was cheaper and I didn't have to color it as often. But before actually making the decision to become a blonde, I decided to buy a blonde wig. Well, I have to tell you that my blonde wig caused heads to turn. People even thought that my husband had a new lady friend. However, when I turned 80, I decided that it was time to let my hair go naturally white. It was a quite nice silvery white.

So back to my present story. When I met Paul I had white hair. Paul, on the other hand, had very nice brown hair at the age of 80. My friends even asked if he dyed his hair, because at 80 you would not expect a male to have naturally brown hair. For Valentine's Day, we chose a Japanese restaurant. I surprised Paul when I appeared wearing my blonde wig. He was in awe. You guessed it. I have been a blonde ever since.

The Three "P's"

Early on in our relationship it was apparent that we would eventually be a couple, barring anything unforeseen. I realize the concern that my family and friends had about our relationship going way too fast. When we were young, most couples were married after an appropriate time of two years into the relationship. But we were in our 80s! We might not have two years. So it was official... Paul and Pris were a couple.

I got a bonus in this newly formed relationship... PIPER! Piper at the time was a 14-year-old loveable mutt. Paul found her at the Lancaster airport thus the name PIPER! When you or your partner decide to move in together, how you treat each other's pets can be a deal breaker. Because if you do not show respect and compassion for the other one's pet, it is never going to work. If my Cody had not passed before I met Paul, I am not sure we would have moved in together so quickly. So we became the three P's … Pris, Paul and Piper. Pets are not the only problem that could affect a relationship.

In the Bedroom

One of the biggest questions that someone reading this book probably would want to know is, do 80-year-olds have sex? The answer is, yes they do.

If you ask a 22-year-old about an 84-year-old having sex, their answer would probably be, "YUCK!" And maybe your answer would be the same. Yes, sex is a part of our lives but only a small part. Arms around me and a sweet goodnight kiss is heavenly bliss to someone my age. Someone to hold the door open for you; squeeze your hand under the table; or just give you a great big smile is enough for me. I am not sure what Paul will say about this subject but I assure you just being considerate of each other, being aware of the other one's feelings is a big "turn on." I do constantly give him compliments, like how good looking he is or what a good job he did on a project. He, on the other hand, tells me how cute I am (which I love to hear being 84 years old), or what a really great dinner I prepared.

Sometimes we do get over-excited, however. It is not all just kissing and hugging. Once I did not realize how close to the edge of the bed Paul was, and I knocked him out into the night stand which had a very sharp edge. Poor Paul, he ended up with a very deep and long gash on his back.

So sex as a senior citizen is not the same as it was when we were in our 30s but love for each other can be demonstrated in many ways.

Early Observations

When we were first together, there was a framed artwork, so to speak, of all of his late wife's blotted lipstick tissues. Paul was convinced that he had created a great piece of artwork and couldn't understand my concern. They were his reminder of his deceased wife. Every morning when I brushed my teeth, I would have to look at those lipstick tissues in a frame because they were right next to my bathroom mirror. Now, you either have to suck it up and ignore it or confront your partner with how you feel. That is what I did and it was taken down immediately.

Another slightly irritating problem is that of being called the wrong name. It happens. I would slip and call him Lee, my last husband's name, instead of Paul. Fortunately, because my voice is so soft, sometimes he would not hear me. He would sometimes call me Grace, his last girlfriend's name. Once in awhile when he got really disgusted about something that I did, he would call me Pam, his daughter's name. But we would just laugh it off and go on about what we were doing.

As for the wedding picture and pictures of other family gatherings posted around the house, I waited until I moved in before discussing their removal. Ultimately, Paul didn't put up too much of an argument about them. He did understand that he needed to let go of his old life. What I was worried about never actually became an issue.

Finances

Finances can be a bone of contention in a relationship, so it is good to have a plan. If both persons have the same income or nearly the same, then combining assets is a good way of working out your finances. However, the alternative is to have a joint account for your monthly expenses and then, if needed, both parties can add more money to the account. This is what Paul and I decided to do. "Money can be the root of all evil," but fortunately that is a perfectly compatible area for us. We just couldn't find anything that caused us to have any major disagreements.

Multi-house Problem

After a year we decided that having two houses is a luxury for the wealthy but not for us. Once you decide to live in one house, then comes the big question: Do you buy into your partner's house or do you just live there rent free? If you have the money, definitely buy into the partner's house. Either way you can get a quitclaim deed.

That is step one. The next step is to see a lawyer. The lawyer will help you both with the general durable power of attorney and the health care power of attorney. I am still thinking about a trust thus preventing a long probate for my kids and partner. When there is a death, relatives pop out of the woodwork. So, as they say in the South, "Get your ducks in a row," and go see an attorney.

PAUL

Initial Impressions of Pawleys Island

Once Pricilla left, I found myself thinking about her all the time. One day went by and we talked on the phone as usual, then another day went by and I missed her even more. Wow! Did I really just spend almost a week basically living with a woman I just met? Yes, and I loved it, and started having very strong feelings for her. I just couldn't wait to see her again. So, after a few days, I said I wanted to come to her house for a visit. That would tell me a lot about her and how she lived. She said she couldn't wait to see me again and that I should come on down. Only a short time had passed, and I was starting to feel I needed to be with her all the time. So I jumped in my car and drove for four hours to her house.

When I walked in I was in awe of how good she looked as she answered the door and how nicely designed her home was. It was very close to a home I would design for myself and, lo and behold, she had designed it herself. Lots of glass, great patios for both indoor and outdoor living. Her house was downright spectacular. I couldn't believe how happy I was to see her. It felt like we had known each other for years, and we were just getting together after a long separation.

Deeper Insights of "Us"

We ate almost all of our meals outside which I thoroughly

enjoyed and we ended up doing it nearly every day. I absolutely loved it. I immediately felt comfortable and it was like we knew each other for years. We drank some wine and relaxed on the sofa and continued the conversation where we left off at my house. The more we talked, the more surprised I was to find out that almost all of her interests were different than mine. Here we are enjoying long conversations about lots of subjects. Religion is very important to her and holds little interest for me. Doing sports like soccer (up until I was 50), mountain climbing, white water rafting, doing triathlons, long-distance running, snow skiing, and scuba diving were things that held my interest. The interesting thing was that, even though she hadn't done most of these activities, she was interested in what I had to say about them, and I was equally interested in the things she had to tell me.

At the same time, she explained her interest in her church and then talked about why it was so important to her. I listened and learned and tried to grasp it. The important thing for both of us is that it doesn't bother me to hear her discuss it, either alone or with her friends. She spent a lot of time talking about her family, her kids and grandkids. They were an interesting bunch. She had a very close relationship with her kids and her grandkids.

Deep inside, she was not a spunky happy girl when we first met, in the sense that she had an older pet dog die suddenly, her husband die after a long illness, and her energetic 99-year-old mother die, all in a very short time frame. She was very close to all of them. She tried to maintain her composure in those early days, but she did struggle with their memories. The good news was that she told me many times that I helped her get over those trying times, and I admitted that she did the same for me.

In my case it was a long period since my wife had died and her memory was starting to fade. My issue was loneliness, because when she was alive, we did everything together, and I had no friends outside of poker, and the poker guys were more like acquaintances than friends. So here we are, enjoying each other's company, talking for hours, and never losing interest in what we have to say.

In Rock Hill there is a giant park called Ann Springs Close Greenway Gardens, with hiking trails, boating, horseback riding, concerts and Sunday Buffet Brunches. We went to many concerts and brunches. It seemed like we just got out of prison. We wanted to get out and do things, and we did. Our lives continued to be happy, it was so nice to have someone to do things with. We found great pleasure in the smallest things. A walk in the park was building a bond between us that could weather any storm. I was feeling stronger and stronger about Pris. We were almost like teenagers, holding hands and stopping for a quick kiss and hug whenever the urge struck us. Life is grand.

Poker and Us

The big sport in my older age is poker. Poker was my only activity until I met Pricilla. I really like to play and she barely knew of its existence. So we spent several nights at home teaching her how to play. I was really surprised that she never even heard of "Texas Hold'em." Teaching her consisted of some education and a lot of fun. She confessed she would never actually play for money, but wanted to understand my biggest interest.

Starting a Tradition

The next time we were at my house, we decided to go out for Valentine's Day. We made reservations and went to a Japanese

Hibachi house and had a great evening. We had a very good time and agreed that that would be an annual dinner for us, and it would be at this restaurant.

After 80 years we both had led full interesting lives. She had three husbands, of which two had died and one ended in divorce. Her life was not pleasant, having had to take care of two very sick husbands, each for many years. I had one wife for 46 years, but we were both healthy and had traveled a lot. I joked often about my chances of having a sudden ailment that made me Husband Number Four that died mysteriously.

Many months have passed. Since then we have spent several weeks at her house at the beach and my house in Rock Hill. We spend nearly every minute together, except for rare commitments from her past. Golf games, bridge, and other forms of idle passing time. We cook meals together, clean up together and enjoy many day trips to learn about each other's current home towns.

Short Periods of Separation

Occasionally we would have periods where for some reason we would be required to spend time alone in our own homes for a few days. I did not like those short periods. But that didn't keep us from being in contact. Most nights we would end our day by getting on "Facetime" and talk with each other while laying in our respective beds. It was not as good as being there in person, but it was better than nothing. We would talk, laugh and carry on until one of our batteries went dead. No, we don't run on batteries, but our phones did! We just never seem to get tired of each other or want to be alone…. I had enough of that over the last ten years.

More about Pawleys Island

The supermarkets and delis were way ahead of Rock Hill. Several of them had a very large selection of excellently prepared meals. This may sound like a bit of trivia, but Rock Hill markets seemed to specialize in wings and other chicken dinners, and all fried. I practically never used them so it wasn't normal for me to run into the supermarket. In Pawleys Island we could get a whole dinner, somewhat healthy, to go. Neither one of us wanted to cook every night.

Along about this time, Pris and I were having fun experimenting with different recipes. Therefore, we were often preparing many of our meals at home. We ate breakfast and lunch on the back patio nearly every day, which usually lasted for hours. I was in heaven. My life had improved about a thousand percent.

She also started telling me she loved me. I thought this was very nice, but although I was feeling very strongly about her, I didn't think it was love yet, so I held back reciprocating. We had only known each other for a few months, and I wasn't sure if I felt that strongly.

Cooking for the Dog

We did everything together. This may sound trite, but after being alone for so long, we really were enjoying each other's company. We cooked doggy meals for my dog Piper. This was a riot. We peeled and sliced a very large amount of sweet potatoes, dried them by laying them on every flat surface we could find in her home, and then baked them in the oven to turn them into doggy potato chips. We had sweet potatoes everywhere there was space to lay them out. The dog loved them, but they ended up being a lot of work as she gobbled them up really fast.

Going to the Country Club

Things were going excellently, and I started spending more and more time at her house. It was summer and I couldn't think of a better place to be. I knew it was inevitable that I was going to meet some of her friends and it was soon to be. Her country club was having its regular monthly dinner dance, and she wanted to go and show me off. I was horrified. This was not my kind of thing. So anyway, I dusted off my closest thing to dressy clothes, my blue blazer. I hadn't worn it in years, and amazingly, it still fit. Then off we went.

When we got to the club, I immediately saw that she knew everybody and was very popular. She introduced me to a huge group of people, whose names I was sure to forget. The good news was that we ended up at the bar and ordered some drinks. I could have used a few more quickly. I was very tense. After we got our drinks we sat down at a table with several couples already there. As she introduced me, she mentioned that three of the men were ex-paratroopers, which made me relax immediately, as I was an old paratrooper myself. The rest of the evening went really well as she had arranged for me to be very comfortable among all of the strangers I was going to meet. Various people came over to the table to say hello to Pris (what everyone called her) and meet me. We even danced a few times and that turned out to not be so bad either. The dance was generally very pleasant and I had a great time, contrary to what I expected.

I came away from that evening with a greater respect for Pris and her compassion for other people after she went to such a significant effort to make sure that we sat at a table where I would be completely comfortable. She knew I would really enjoy being at a table full of crazy paratroopers.

After such a good start with her friends, we generally lived life as any reasonably normal people. Friends came over the house for drinks; we had small parties; and I generally got to know many of her friends quite well. We were invited out for drinks or for dinner many times and I really liked that, because the restaurants in her beach town were much better than what was available in Rock Hill. Her friends had fun and so did we. I even liked her friends and became quite comfortable around them.

A New Bank Account

We went to the bank and opened a joint account so that we could share the expenses that we incurred going out to dinner (we did that a lot), buying groceries and whatever came up. Each month we would each put an equal amount of money in the account and use it until it was empty. Then we would do it again as many times as we needed. We didn't have a clue how much money we needed each month, but we didn't want either of us to bear the burden of all of it. It worked out real well, and we still are using that account in the same way for our regular household expenses today.

Learn about the City

We took a guided tour of her city, went to Brookgreen Gardens and did about everything there was to do and see around Pawleys Island. We were growing together more and more each day and I didn't think that anything could separate us. I was committed and she was, too. Brookgreen gardens was a giant private park with farm animals, unusual vegetation, and lectures on nature. It also had alligators. Lots and lots of alligators. One must keep his eyes moving on a swivel at all times or risk becoming dinner for a lurking beast. Not the best of experiences for me.

Poker with the Neighbors

In the time I stayed at Pris's house, I got friendly with the neighbor and he mentioned that he played poker on Friday nights with a group of local guys. I asked if I could join them and so I made some new friends. It was a very low-cost game, and they were terrible players. I won all the money every time I went and started to feel guilty, because my skill level was far greater than any of theirs. But the game was only second to the good time we all had. So I got a night out without Pris and... it felt strange.

A Day at the Beach

We went to the beach, and Pris said she had body surfed often, so we bought a couple of body boards and jumped in the ocean and caught a few waves. This was a major effort by Pris, as she does not swim at all. She did wear a flotation device, but that had limited capabilities in a very strong surf. After all went well for the first few waves, it was no big surprise that finally a really big wave came along and threw us up on the beach in a tangled up mess. We were laughing our heads off as several young people ran over to save us. All said the same thing: They hoped they could do what we do at our age. We just watched the surf for a while, got our equilibrium back and went home after a big workout, still laughing about it. I admired Pris a great deal for her courage and willingness to jump in a turbulent ocean as a non-swimmer.

We didn't turn the TV on much, I guess both of our lives got more interesting. After dinner we talked a long time and then went to bed, where I continued to amaze both her and me at my new-found energy. If you all think that finding an 80-plus-year-old sexy is not possible, let me be the first to say you're wrong! We were constantly amazed at our energy levels.

Local Chili Contest and Beer Festival

We went to an annual beer and chili festival one Sunday and ate much too much chili and drank a lot of beer. I usually don't drink beer. They had bagpipers marching around and playing music. Just another good time doing nothing special. We did laugh a lot and enjoy ourselves doing the simplest things. I really enjoyed this and had a great time trying to pick the best chili out of many good chili bowls. The local people were very friendly and it was an ideal day, good food, lots of beer, and lots of fun on this bright sunny day.

Multi-house Problem

We carried on our relationship for several months this way and started talking about living together. The problems we faced were which house to stay in? Buy a new house near her daughter or buy one in Rock Hill. In closing this segment, let me point out that the time period discussed above was approximately six months. I really liked staying at the beach and would have been very happy living in her home, but I also like my home. There was really nothing holding me there, so I was wide open to Pris's thoughts on the subject. Well, we were full of great ideas and had a long and happy life on the horizon, but along came Covid and things would change.

A Visit to Her Lawyer

Not everything we did was fun and games. As we felt we were getting serious with each other for the long term, we knew we had to address how all of our plans would affect our families. An issue that was bothering Pris was being on my home's title if she moved in. So we went to see her local lawyer and asked him to verify that what I had told her about just simply putting her on my title via a quitclaim deed without her putting up any money would solve her concern. I told her I didn't need or want her money. She could be on the title at no out-of-pocket expense. She had a hard time grasping this even after the lawyer blessed it. So she eventually bought half of my home for cash.

We also made up new living wills, medical power, etc., to cover us for the future in our new life. This was all pretty straightforward. Of course the lawyer loved the work and he generated a large pile of paper for each of us. Pris had the big decisions to make, because her daughter was executor of most things and she had to figure out how I was going to fit in to that big picture.

Chapter 4
MEETING THE KIDS

PRIS

Meeting the family for the first time is a very dramatic experience for both parties. I was especially nervous since this is my fourth partner. Jenny (my daughter) grew to love my last husband, Lee, and now I had to get her to love Paul. The first meeting was at a restaurant with just my daughter. I can't say that it was a great success because Jenny was not ready for me to have another man in my life... however, later we were invited to my daughter's home at Lake Norman and it was a very pleasant evening. She made s'mores over their open fire pit. I think that was Paul's first taste of s'mores, and he was certainly not eager to taste them again. Now, three years later, the family has accepted him and he loves my family.

Since he does not have any grandchildren, he especially enjoys my twin grandchildren. He has yet to meet my other two grandchildren who live far from us. The twins are in their thirties. One just graduated from Princeton with a PhD in anthropology. The other twin graduated from Yale law school and now is at MIT studying political science. They are both very knowledgeable and interesting to engage in conversation, so Paul certainly enjoys their presence. If the family is not overwhelmingly accepting of your new partner, my advice is to be patient. The family will probably come around at some point. And if they don't... that is their loss! The main thing is that you do not let your children interfere with your happiness!

I have yet to meet any of Paul's family. His efforts to contact them, both by phone or internet have not resulted in any communications with them since his wife's death. I am praying that this will change before it is too late. Recently I have convinced him to make another effort at contacting them.

PAUL

We had another big step coming up in our relationship. Meeting the first of her kids, Pris's daughter Jennifer. When Pris told me her daughter's age (59), it reminded me of my age, as I didn't think of myself as old, even though I was 81. I noticed, and I have heard other older folks say the same thing. They didn't see themselves as much different than they had been during their 20s or 30s. I felt the same way. However, the aches and pains that we experience don't let us totally forget it.

First Meeting with Jennifer

We met Jennifer at the Fish Market restaurant in Rock Hill for the first time. As I remember I didn't get to talk too much, as is probably pretty normal when mother and daughter get together. I also think Jenny didn't want to seem like she was prying. The first thing I noticed was that she hardly ate anything, which probably accounted for her thinness. Anyway, she was a very likeable person and I felt that we would have a good relationship. This was when it became obvious that anything of any significance we discussed at home would be repeated in detail to Jennifer.

54

Another idiosyncrasy I discovered about Pris was that she really wanted to brag about me to people I was just meeting. At the slightest notion, she would say "Oh, Paul was a paratrooper" or "Paul sailed around the world in his own boat," etc., etc. Now, I feel like these are things for me to bring up, if I feel that the occasion is right. This always embarrasses me and makes me uncomfortable. I do know that most people generally aren't interested in your more youthful adventures anyway. It makes me feel awkward to discuss them, which I inevitably end up doing. I mentioned my feelings about this and she agreed that sometimes she just felt so proud about what an exciting guy I was that she couldn't resist bragging. She promised to try real hard not to do it anymore. This was the first time we had any issue to discuss other than our lives now and in the future.

Meeting Son-in-Law for the First Time

The next time we met Jennifer again and Ken for the first time was at their house in Charlotte. They lived in an exclusive area close to downtown. If it sounded like I was anxious about meeting her friends at the country club, that was nothing compared to my anxiety for this meeting. Her daughter lived close to us and I knew we would be seeing a lot of them. Pris had told me quite a bit about them, so I felt a little prepared in what I should expect.

They had fraternal twins, both of whom were very smart and were going for their doctorates. This was going to at least give us something in common (not the very smart part), as I was an identical twin myself. They wouldn't be here for our first get-together, because both of them lived out of state, so we would just be meeting Jenny (for me, the second time) and her husband Ken.

When we arrived, we were greeted warmly. I couldn't help but think that Jennifer was thinking of me as some type of weirdo hnging on to her reasonably well-off Mother. Pris had had one bad relationship when she moved too fast after her first husband died. It would be reasonable for Jenny to feel that her Mom might be moving too fast again. But Jenny didn't appear that way to me as we sat out on the back patio and roasted s'mores.

I never particularly cared for roasted s'mores, and was thinking to myself that she probably thinks of us as kids.

The good news was she also had homemade pizzas with unusual toppings on them, and specifically had them because Pris had mentioned that I loved pizza. The pizza was delicious and as we relaxed a bit, the evening went really well. I sensed that Jennifer was just as nervous as I was, and it took her a little while to relax, as it did me. Ken was pretty quiet during the evening. He was an executive in his company and probably kept his current problems at the office in the back of his mind. I remember that I was like that when I worked as an executive in some high tech companies in California. He still exhibits some of that quietness when we get together. All in all, the first get-together seemed to go quite well and as time went on, I felt very close to them.

Pris will eventually move into my house to be closer to them. As it turns out, they decided to move to a new house at one of the lakes surrounding Charlotte, and it will take a little more time to visit them. But it was not a problem for us.

Jennifer is very aware of her mother's age and wanted to see her often. Not only visits, but frequent phone calls as well. I thought this was really nice and it gave me a very high opinion of her, especially when considering how my kids act towards me. We see them often and always have a pleasant time. Jenny is a very good cook as well.

Meeting John

Pris had two children. Along with Jenny, she had a younger son named John. Pris talked to John on the phone quite often and occasionally I would listen to their conversations, which made me feel like I knew him already. He lived in Kansas and has a high level job that keeps him from visiting often. But he finally came to South Carolina for a long weekend. John was a Type One diabetic with many additional problems generated from his diabetes. He seemed to be a quiet guy and liked to be by himself, but he appeared to accept me and was glad that his mother had found me. I found him to be a likeable guy and I hope he can join us again soon. So now I had met the immediate family and felt that there would not be any problems in our future.

(left to right) Paul, Pris, Jenny and John

Jennifer Plans our Future

As time marches on, Pris and I have had many discussions about some ideas that Jennifer has been suggesting for us. Remember, we are both independent people, and Pris has indicated that Jenny has brought up the subject of our moving closer to them more than once. She even went as far as picking out a condo that she thought we would just love near where they are living now.

What I see as a potential problem could be down the road a short distance. Jenny and Ken have two kids in their early 30s, and both are getting serious about their lady friends. Jenny has indicated that she might want to move close to any grandchildren when the time comes. Now I know from past friends that this is a pretty standard way of thinking for most women. Grandkids or great-grandkids are the Gold Standard for women in general, and nothing can stop them when it comes to being around these kids as much as possible, including moving next door. So why do we care?

Now this may never be a problem for us, but we have our own plans that don't involve any moves in the future. Money is not an issue for us, and traveling on airlines is less and less appealing to either one of us as we get older. Long drives already do not appeal to me. We think all of this could become a problem in the future. Pris feels very strongly about seeing her daughter no matter where she lives and she probably will want to be around her great-grandkids when they do arrive. I wouldn't mind being close to them myself, but the last thing I want to do is move out of the home we are living in right now. I have several friends I know currently who live in Rock Hill only because they moved here to be close to one of their kids. Then after a very short time, the kids moved far away because of career opportunities.

We Don't Need No Stinking Old Folks Home

We have spent a considerable amount of time planning and preparing for our later years. We have converted our garage into a one-bedroom apartment. It has everything in it we would need for day-to-day living, including no steps anywhere. We expect that we will either move into the garage apartment or give it to someone in exchange for some light caregiving and light cooking and cleaning. We could also just rent out whichever one of the units we are not using and pay for in-home care. We do know that down the road we will probably have to have some kind of help.

Chapter 5

COVID COMES TO TOWN

PRIS

We met in January and the Covid pandemic started in March. It was a difficult time for everyone. Husbands and wives were working from their homes, so they were together 24/7. One could not go anywhere there were other people that you did not want to expose yourself to. There were those who might not be vaccinated. Paul and I were pretty much housebound so we had to find our own self-entertainment.

Dancing at Home

Tango was our first attempt at home entertainment. We found instructions on YouTube and we did fairly well, except for Paul's four feet. Most of the time we were laughing so hard that we had to sit down. So our tango lessons were short lived.

Playing Cards

Cards were our next form of entertainment. Paul taught me how to play Texas Hold'em and I taught him Phase 10. If you know anything about Phase 10, you know there are 10 sets. The first time he played, he won all 10 sets! In Texas Hold'em I faired a little bit better, even though Paul had placed in the money in several tournaments, including the World Championship in Las Vegas.

Piano

But the exciting thing I think for both of us was when I taught him how to play the piano. Paul had a Yamaha keyboard boxed up in his tool shed. I asked Paul about it. He said that he had wanted to learn to play the piano but had just never gotten around to it. It had been several years since I had played the piano but if he wanted to learn I could brush up on my piano skills. So the lessons began. He had trouble remembering which key was "A" and which key was "C," so I ordered letters that he could stick on the keyboard, which helped him immensely. Soon he was actually playing melodies. Hearing him play "When the Saints Come Marching In" was music to my ears!

We Can Cook

Both of us enjoy cooking. When he told me that he could cook, I replied, "I've never had a man who cooked." "How often do I have to cook," he asked. "Well," I replied, "there are seven days a week and three meals a day." There was dead silence at the other end of the phone. This was before we even met. But we do take turns cooking. We even cooked for our dog. We peeled, dried, and baked about 12 sweet potatoes for our precious Piper. There were drying sweet potatoes in every space available.

Learning Stock Options

Finally, the item that almost caused me to pack up and go back to the beach was STOCK OPTIONS! Paul is active in trading options. He even taught option classes. Me... I was never a math student. I taught interesting subjects like American history, Spanish, and English. So numbers were and are a complete disaster for me. And this is where I found out one of Paul's failures. He is IMPATIENT! "Why can't you understand this?" He would ask. With that, I would run out of the room in tears. I was to find out more about his impatient nature throughout our relationship. But then none of us is perfect. In the end I told him, "No options for me!"

Like everyone else we managed to get through the pandemic but with a few scars. I think the most difficult thing for me was being in a new place and knowing no one but Paul. At the beach, I had been Miss Socializer.

A Little Surprise

One day I noticed a bird nest in the hanging plant on our front porch. We watched the eggs hatch into little peeping birds. As we watched, we noticed that the mama bird had not returned and some of the weaker babies had died. We looked up on the internet to find out what to feed the baby birds. We fed them with an eye dropper. Alas, only one little bird survived.
One time when we went to feed him, he had fallen out of the nest into the bush below the nest. He still was not able to fly so he hopped out of the bush. Suddenly from a bush in the middle of our yard came a sound from an adult bird. The little bird peeped a response. This kept up until the baby bird reached the adult bird. The baby bird's little wings flapped with joy when the two birds met. It almost made us cry to see their joy.

Adventure on the Catawba River

I am what you would call a very cautious person. I would

not fly in a small plane. I do not go on "down" escalators, unless forced, and I would never go past the second step on a ladder. So one summer day, when we were having a lovely lunch at the Pump House, which overlooks the Catawba River, we saw hundreds of people floating peacefully in their tubes. It seemed a natural idea that Paul suggested that we try that sport. As I looked down on the "tubers" and saw little children and even some toddlers, it seemed like a non-threatening adventure.

Since it was the pandemic and tubing was the one sport families could do together, there were no tubes to be found... not even online! Of course, rentals of such were not allowed due to the pandemic. Fortunately, when walking one day with my neighbor, she informed me that she had two tubes and she would be happy to lend them to us.

The day came and we went to the store to buy a pump to fill our tubes with air, put them in the trunk of our car, and scurry to the dam at Ft. Mill where we would launch them. The first thing that I noticed was that we seemed to be the oldest ones there by 50 years at least, which should have given me some hesitation about that upon which we were about to embark. I also noticed that I had more of my body covered up than anyone else.

Have your ever seen an 81-year-old try to get into a tube? Believe me, it is not a pretty sight. Finally we were comfortably in our tubes floating down the great Catawba River. I use the word "comfortable" loosely. Sitting in five inches of water is not exactly a comfortable feeling. The sun was out and everyone on the river seemed to be having a good time. Paul said, "Isn't this great!" And it was so relaxing... the first hour. Did I mention that the temperature that day was in the 90s? Did I also mention that we did not put on or bring with us any type of sun protection? After two hours I thought I smelled burning flesh. It was about this time that I noticed that Paul's expression on his face did not emanate that this tubing adventure was so great. It was also about this time that Paul gave up on trying to give me instructions on which way I should steer. Ooh! That's right. We did not have any oars like the other tubers. We used our hands, and I could never get it straight which way I was supposed to swish them through the water to go the right way. It was also about the same time we came upon a large group of rocks sticking up out of the water, with some that were submerged just far enough under the surface that you could not see them until you were right there. Of course, you guessed it. I ended up on top of a big rock which was a few inches below the surface. Try as we might Paul and I could not move my bottom off the rock. Finally, Paul got out of his tube and pushed me off the rock. It was interesting to note that none of those youngsters tubing down the river came to the aid of their elders.

Finally after four, yes, four hours of tubing, we came in sight of our disembarking point. It was at this time I asked Paul about the key to the car that we had carefully wrapped in a baggie and sealed. He looked around and finally remembered that he had put it in his swimming suit pocket. Alas! he had gotten in the water to get me off the rock forgetting about the car key in his pocket. When he found it, the seal had broken. Disembarking from our tubes was even more difficult than getting into our tubes at the beginning of the trip. Hot, tired and burned to a crisp, we retrieved our lunch and were proud that we had accomplished such a feat and were relieved that it was over! And thankfully, our car key still worked. In the weeks that followed Paul and I experienced our first sunburn peel in at least 30 years!

The Project

Men beware! Women will immediately want to change things. And I am afraid to say it, but I was no different. We called it THE PROJECT! Our eating area was about 2 x 4 feet which allowed a very small table and two chairs. The two narrow windows looked out onto a forest of 100+ acres. But, our view was limited. "Why don't we build a nook," I asked. "Well, I have often thought about it," he replied. The next thing you know, we had a nook and 10 feet added to our deck. Paul, at 81, did most of the work. However, I do not recommend this because Paul did take a fall and broke in two an aluminum leveler. During this time we set up a small table in the corner of the living room. Because this was in a dark corner of the room, we had to use candles. So romantic! I enjoy our beautiful view now of the woods behind our house, but I also miss our romantic candlelight dinners.

PAUL

We were spending more time at my home. When Covid came along, because of our ages, we decided to get the shots, boosters, etc. Fortunately for us, Rock Hill was a small enough town that we basically drove up, got our shots in the car and waited fifteen minutes to see if there was any reaction. If not, we drove home. This was very quick and easy. Of course we had all the worries that everyone seemed to be having, with all the confusion about whether they worked or not. So we agreed that we would add the safety measure of staying home as much as possible.

Some might think that too much togetherness might be very dangerous for a new relationship. Being together every minute might have us start getting on each other's nerves. But the opposite happened; we got closer and closer, which was fine with me.

The first thing we didn't do was watch TV all the time. We spent a lot of time in the kitchen preparing meals from interesting recipes taken from the internet. I learned about the foods she ate when she was growing up, and she did the same. For me that was basic Eastern European, Polish and Hungarian. My father's mother was Polish and my mother's family was Hungarian. My father's mother was alive while I was growing up and she cooked for us occasionally, while my mother who did most of the cooking in my youth, cooked from her mother's cookbook. Pris's primary style was based on Ohio cookery and Southern cooking. She had lived in the South a lot longer than I.

Playing the Piano

I had an electric piano stored in the garage. I dragged it into the house, where I started trying to advance past the point I had gotten to after I first bought it. I didn't expect any miracles because I have always been tone deaf and that didn't change as I got older. Lo and behold! Pris was quite good on the piano, so she spent some time getting her skill back and then teaching me enough to get me past where I had left off years ago. Needless to say, we had a lot of fun with this and we both spent a great deal of time playing (or trying to play). I will never be a famous pianist.

Cooking

I guess the first mistake I made was cooking Pris an exotic meal on our first date. She wasn't crazy about the Ma Poa Bean Curd, but she really loved some of my other dishes. Her favorite is Chinese-style lemon chicken served with fried rice. She couldn't get enough of it. I didn't mind so much because it was delicious, and I could eat it very often myself. So when we eventually started having guests, she would ask me to make it. I would say I will have to add some dishes, because one dish is not enough. What would they be? How about Hot and Sour soup, Ma Poa Bean Curd (you heard about this from our first date) and maybe fried rice and pot stickers.

I should mention that I took advanced Chinese cooking classes in California. I did it because I love Chinese food and wanted to learn how to make a full repertoire of meals. Now that I live in South Carolina, it's amazing how many folks we meet that never heard of most things I am good at cooking. That doesn't mean I don't cook them; I just feed guests a lot of wine. That loosens them up about the food, and they become more relaxed about eating it. Anyway, I am the official cook when we have company, and I enjoy doing it. In this house the cook normally doesn't clean up.

Pris is a very good cook in her own right. She makes meals from really old cookbooks that have been handed down for many generations. The only problem being that a lot of the methods use very old-fashioned methods and ingredients, many of them being unhealthy. They also don't mention air fryers or microwaves, etc. at all. But she is also getting quite adept at finding yummy meals on the internet. In any case, her cooking is good, and I am happy to have her prepare a meal.

One of the other things I like to do occasionally is look on the internet for foods I grew up with. Things like New York pizza, pretzels, knishes, rice balls and lots more. It's amazing how many cooks are making shortcut versions of these foods, making it hard to find authentic versions of the foods from my youth.

Learning Poker

She was also intrigued by another hobby of mine. We spent hours playing poker on the kitchen table with seven dummies to make it more interesting. Using the dummies made the practice more interesting because we could simulate a full table of players. But the problem with using dummies is that they don't do the things a real poker player would do. It's hard to teach someone "Texas Hold'em" with only two players, so I played seven hands against Pris which gave her the big picture. It was fun and she got to know what I was talking about when I said things like, "My straight was beat by a flush on the river." When I did eventually go to a live game, she would know why the details affected me, and not just stare at me with a blank look on her face.

Pris Learns Stock Options

The biggest thing we did together, which in hindsight we should not have done at all, was attempting to teach Pris "Stock Option Trading." She had several stock accounts and felt she would understand the course. After all, she had earned a Masters degree with honors.

I have been trading options for about 30 years and am pretty much of an expert on them. So a bunch of years back, I developed a 24-chapter course on how to trade options and made them available on CDs to the general public. They are not for stock market beginners! So as happened with the piano and poker, Pris decided she wanted to know all about them. I was against it, but she insisted. So I gave her a CD and let her do the entire course by herself. I was not surprised when she said she did not understand a few things, so we started going through the course together. Most of the course flew over her head, and it turns out she didn't understand anything at all. I tried over and over to illustrate how they worked, but the "light" never came on. Her frustration and my natural impatience caused tears to flow, but she didn't want to give up. More tears flowed and even more tears flowed. I was feeling awful and was just as anxious for her to understand them as she was to learn them, so I didn't want to give up either.

Even when we started trading options live with real money, she could not follow what was happening. She liked the part about making money, so we tried to continue. More tears! Finally we agreed this was not for her, and I would trade until everything was closed out and then we would stop. Smiles! This was a close call and pretty much the only negative thing that occurred in our early relationship. She was not happy and totally frustrated. I was glad when we stopped the training and got on with our lives. The good thing about Pris is her ability to let bad things go and see the good side of everything, which she had to do with great vigor in this case. So you've heard the worst. Now for the best, but not just one best.

Dancing at Home

One evening we watched a movie called "Assassination Tango" with one of my favorite actors starring in it, Robert Duvall. It was about a New York gangster who gets a contract to kill a politico in South America. He must wait for final approval, so he wanders around the city and sees people dancing the tango through the window of a Tango school, and he goes in and starts learning himself.

The music and the grace of the dancers really moved both of us, so when the movie was over, we went on line and found a class on learning the Tango for beginners. It was really fun. I'm no dancer, but we really enjoyed doing this. We danced and moved through the lessons many nights and had the most fun I have had with a woman out of bed in many years. Tired of TV every night? Try Tango lessons to beef up your relationship.

The Kitchen Nook Project

The best thing was a giant project, which in large part consumed whole days for many months and was a true togetherness effort, with the culmination in the evening (sort of). My kitchen eating area was tiny and we had a very small round table in it. It was so small, we could only place two plates on it with nothing extra. It also blocked the path between several rooms, even though it was tiny.

Pris mentioned it would be nice if we could expand the eating area. I answered that I had been thinking about doing it for years. It looked like an easy project. Several weeks and it would be done. I started drawing up plans to expand the eating area into our backyard. It also required the disassembling of the old deck. We would add on a new deck on the other side of the future new wall. We agreed on my plan and Pris looked the design over. She wanted several changes – the biggest one being the size of the new room. She said adding square feet was not a big deal before the project was underway, but it would be impossible later as the project moved along and we wanted a change. So we made it bigger. What else? We agreed that we should do it, and we got started immediately.

Pris also suggested that if I'm doing the physical work, she would pay for the materials. I objected since I thought of us as a family that shared everything. Well, she insisted because she had a pile of money from the sale of her house, and she could afford it more easily. That's hard to object to. She said we would have to pay people to do it if I didn't, so she won.

The majority of the work was a do-it-yourself project of the kind I love to do. I have done add-ons and modifi-cations to every house I have lived in, so this was not new to me. The problem now became where to eat our meals and our solution was almost the best part of the proj-ect – more on this in a bit.

I got the plans approved by the county and started making a materials list. I did this so I could get everything delivered at once. Delivery fees are killers. As I started to knock down the old outside wall, I saw another side of Pris that I had not seen before. Fear....Fear of me hurting myself tearing out the wall, lifting heavy beams, going up ladders, etc. Her favorite expression became, "Can't we have that done by a professional, or isn't that a good job for a handyman?" I kept explaining that I had done many projects like this over my lifetime and didn't have any problems. But she kept it up and I finally started sending her on errands to get something I needed so that I could finish what I was doing. Then I could get the work done without her standing there watching me and wringing her hands. Well, one day when I was working on the upper portion of the walls, one of the legs of the ladder I was standing on slipped off the beam it was resting on, and I came tumbling down. I didn't stop at the floor because there wasn't any, so I kept going to the dirt about 3 feet below where the floor would eventually go. The good news was that my brand new six-foot aluminum level was laying across the beams and I hit it square on. So the level stopped my fall a little, but it was completely ruined after it folded in half. I was home alone, so I lay there a few minutes and – oh no! Pris came home and gave me the "I told you so" look. Nothing serious was wrong and after a short break, I got back to work with an aching hip.

My house has a big dining room, but the table and chairs and everywhere in between was filled with unpacked boxes from Pris's upcoming move. We had a good solution. We moved the little table from the kitchen to the living room, in which one corner was empty. Our kitchen table would fit in it nicely, so that's where it went. There was no light nearby, so we agreed that we would eat by candlelight. I thought it would be difficult to do every night, but it wasn't and it was actually fun. We talked a lot and it was very relaxing. It was also quite romantic. Lots of folks thought this project was going to put a large stress on our relationship. It did just the opposite, again. We became even more romantic. We definitely did not act like the seniors we were. The romantic part was great. When we passed each other in the kitchen or hallway, we always stopped for a hug or a hug and a kiss, or several. We were like teenagers. We had both suffered

through some traumas not that long ago, and we both felt that this style of life would definitely enhance our feelings for each other. Not that we discussed them all the time, it's just that we were feeling very comfortable about each other, and the hugs and kisses became a natural part of our day.

All these hugs and kisses didn't

Our temporary dining area

73

start with the new construction project. It started when we were near each other for any reason, right from the beginning. Pris is a lot warmer, sensitive and more loving person than I am, but

as time went by, it rubbed off on me. I enjoyed all the physical closeness, and it led to the bedroom more often than seemed possible at our age. This was definitely the good life and I was going to tread lightly to make sure it didn't change.

So, I was busy during the day hammering away on the project outside, and then would come in at lunchtime for something to eat and a little rest. Some of the work required a younger body, like putting on the new roof and I had found the perfect contractor to help. He didn't mind doing a piece of the work here and there, and he was not that expensive. This allowed the project to move pretty quickly.

Pris Overcomes Her Fear of Heights

Another part of the project also had a big effect on Pris. I knew that she was afraid of heights and wouldn't even ride an

The finished project

escalator or go up a ladder higher than the second step from the bottom. Well, occasionally I had to position large ceiling beams on top of the new walls and couldn't hold both ends up by myself. So Pris got volunteered (sort of like the Army) on many occasions, and she went up very high on one of the ladders. She did this several times. After a while, the complaining and fearful view of what she did didn't cause as much agony on her part as she showed in the beginning. The project ended after about six months, and we both are very pleased with the outcome. Of course, she still talks about her fear of heights.

We also had many meals by candlelight in the new room

because we haven't forgotten the pleasure we both got from the time we basically had to do it. It's a great way to end our busy day of outside activities and a quiet time for us as a couple.

It was nice that this occurred at the same time Covid was slowing down. Neither of us had caught it up to this point, so we started going out more. Pris joined the New-

Pris faces her fear of heights

comers Club and got busy really fast; she started playing golf and bridge every week. There were meetings for this or that very often.

She also restarted her card-making business and showed her skills at various local craft fairs. People like her cards, and she always sells most of them. We will not get rich from this endeavor, but she enjoys doing it. I joined the YMCA and started going regularly for a workout and swim. We were meeting new people and started having people over for dinner or going out to dinner with new friends.

Floating Down the Catawba River

A really big thing for us was to get some float tubes and go down the Catawba River one Sunday. This was a very big thing for Pris as she is a non-swimmer. The trip is a very mellow way to spend a day and we enjoyed ourselves immensely. Of course, we were the only ones on the river above the age of 30. The whole trip required very little effort because we just let the current carry us down the river. The fast water was not very fast, so it was a big surprise that after a while Pris managed to get herself grounded on a big rock sticking out of the water. She didn't show much fear as we worked to get her free. It was like watching Laurel and Hardy with the two of us bumping into each other with the cumbersome tubes and extra life vest Pris had on. We were laughing very hard, so no one on the river thought we were in real trouble and, of course, we weren't. It didn't take long to undo ourselves, and other rafters didn't even seem to notice two 80-year-olds performing a comedy routine for them. The pleasure of the trip down the river was somewhat nullified by the sunburns we both got. We did lather ourselves up with sunscreen, but it wore off after awhile and we suffered for several days before we stopped peeling. We did enjoy the trip and would do it again with hats and umbrellas – items we didn't think to bring on this trip.

During Covid, the only folks we saw outside of our home were Pris's daughter and family. Things always went well, and we always enjoyed ourselves when they visited us or we visited them. On rare occasions we would go out to dinner with some folks from the Newcomers Club, but not too often because everyone was still afraid of getting sick.

So for us, Covid wasn't the end of the world, it was a way for us to really spend a lot of quality time together. It shortened the time it would normally take for us to get to know each other well. But that did not mean there were no surprises in the near future.

Chapter 6

THE BIG PLAN – MERGING HOUSEHOLDS

PRIS

Going back and forth from Rock Hill and Pawleys Island became an arduous 4-hour trip. I could not remember in which house I had ketchup or milk. So Paul and I decided not to keep both houses. Since my daughter lived close to Paul and since I was "old" and she wanted me near her, we decided to make Paul's house our home. I was able to sell my house for twice the price that I paid for it. Thus, on December 17, 2020, the moving truck arrived and loaded up all my belongings. The following day they unloaded it at Paul's house in Rock Hill.

Usually when one moves into a new house, it is into an empty house. In our case, merging the two households would not be an easy task. Paul was very considerate and not only said that I could do anything I wanted to fix up the house, he MEANT it! Of course, his man cave (shop and tool shed) was off limits. However, I have had friends who moved into their partner's house but were not allowed to make any changes, thus making the woman feel like it was never her house.

My mother was an interior decorator, and she said that her most difficult jobs were the "merging households." The couple would say, "Anything is okay to get rid of." But when the time came that my mother would suggest that a piece of furniture or a lamp would not fit in… "Oh no that was my grandmother's." Paul proved true to his word. My dining room set was a little higher quality, so we put his on Marketplace on Facebook and sold it. Also his desk ensemble was about to fall apart, so he took mine for his office. We kept his more comfortable living room and bedroom set, although I did bring my bedroom chest. An important thing, ladies or gentlemen… purchase a new mattress! Even though it had been eight years since anyone had slept on my side of the bed, it just felt a little weird. I did bring my own washer and dryer which was newer than his by a whole lot of years. Another aspect of merging households that you don't think about is the little things like silverware, dishes, pots and pans, spices, etc. We now have four sets of China, two sets of pottery, and six sets of silverware. We also have three containers of spices. I would like to have used the past tense, however, we still have all of the above-mentioned.

Now ladies, we discuss the closet details. I had had a whole walk-in closet all to myself and so had Paul. We needed to divide the closet in his home in half. To this day he lets me know if my hanger is on his side. Fortunately for me, he had made his garage into a nice little apartment with a very nice walk-in closet. After adding another hanging bar in the "cottage," as we call it, we provided a great place for my off-season clothes.

I might mention that before I moved into Paul's house, I had a she-shed built, and it was a brilliant move on my part. It was a place that I could keep some things that were dear to me but not necessarily functional. So you can see that there are some problems in merging households, but having someone to share your life with is greater than any piece of furniture. Although I still hear from time to time, "Do you really need this?"

To Be or Not to Be... Married

To be married or not to be? That is the question. There are several reasons that people choose to live together but not be married. Those reasons are magnified for seniors. If the previous spouse died, then the living person could lose their spouse's pension, social security or medical insurance. However, sometimes it is not financial but has to do with family situations. The children of the spouse might worry that the current friend might be after their parent's money. One might think that this is very selfish on the children's part, but I feel that it is a very valid concern and should not be dismissed lightly.

Paul and I decided not to get married but live as domestic partners for life. The reason is one that I mentioned previously, loss of insurance. He was on his wife's insurance policy and, if he would get married again, he would lose it. Since it was unbelievably good insurance, it would be a sin to not keep it, especially at our age. However, last Christmas, Paul gave me a beautiful small band of sapphires and diamonds ring. We call it the promise ring. Just absolutely beautiful! He even got down on his knee and asked me to marry him, just like in the movies. So romantic! I really don't know why I felt the necessity for a ring. We had already committed ourselves to each other forever. But having a ring on my finger just felt GOOD! This was three years after we met.

There is another way to be together. Sometimes religion plays a big part in the decision whether to marry or not. I have a relative that is a very strong Christian. After her husband died, she met a gentleman. They fell in love. Again, financially they could not get married because she would lose her late husband's pension but she did not feel right about living with a man without being married. She talked to her minister about it. He suggested that she receive God's blessing in a private ceremony, sanctioned by God but not the state. It is not easy to find a minister that is willing to do this, but it is worth looking into. I know you are asking why Paul and I did not do this.

I had been brought up as a Presbyterian. As a teenager I was very active in my church. I was even chosen as the one person to represent the state of Kansas in a national youth conference in Estes Park, Colorado. When I moved to Myrtle Beach, I was very active in the church there, serving as moderator of the ladies' groups and as shepherd deacon.

Paul was brought up in the Catholic religion. He received some of his education in Catholic schools. But along the way, he became disenchanted with religion and no longer was a Believer. Therefore, having a church blessing would have been a sham. I believe that as long as Paul's views do not in any way cause me to stumble and lose my belief in God, that I can stay with him forever. He has been very considerate and has even been supportive in accompanying me in some of the church's activities.

PAUL

Life was moving along very nicely and we were enjoying each other with no signs of anything that would cause all of this good living to end. I was now sure that I was in love with Pris, and I was comfortable in knowing that she was in love with me. We had to start planning a real life together and move from a casual relationship to a long-term commitment.

The interesting question that bothered Pris was how we called each other. Do we say, This is my wife Pris, or meet my husband Paul, or are we partners, or spouses? The worst one we heard about was, "This is my special friend." It's almost laughable at our age. I liked going with husband and wife. After all, they are only words anyway, sanctioned by paying a government fee. It mattered little to me. She understood that at our age our lives will become much more complicated. Our decisions didn't only impact us but our immediate family as well. She was close to her family and I had no concerns for mine. All of Bonnie's family was dead, and my kids didn't know if I was alive or dead.

Pris's concern was more based on how she was seen in the eyes of God. Because this was a small issue to me and a big one to her, I let her decide.

We met in January 2020 and, after six months or so, we decided to discuss selling one of our houses. We both were getting tired of the commute back and forth to Rock Hill and Pawleys Island. This was not an easy decision. We both liked each house, but for different reasons. Her house was really nicely set up and comfortable. She had all her friends there that she had known for a really long time. It was a very prestigious address being right on the beach and all. The only negative about Pris's house was it was very close to the main road in Pawleys Island and very noisy from traffic. In the winter we didn't hear anything because the windows were closed.

On the other hand, I really didn't have any friends in Rock Hill. My house was older and, although it was nicely decorated, it didn't stand out as anything special. It was nice because it was on an acre of property and very private. I also had a reverse mortgage on it that would have to be paid off along with its accumulated interest. For those out there who think there is some kind of government conspiracy connected with reverse mortgages, let me give you first-hand knowledge that there isn't! They are good because you can get a big lump of cash or regular payments made to you from the bank that writes the loan. You don't have to pay it back until you sell your home, which in my case I had planned for it to be after I die. A great deal if you need more money to live on and you are not worried about your heirs (remember my kids from the preface). Anyway, I didn't have enough cash to pay the loan off.

So after much hand-wringing, we decided to sell Pris's house. She had planned to sell her house before we met and move near her daughter, anyway; she just kind of let the time pass without doing it. We knew we wanted to live together no matter what, so we made a plan. We put her house on the market and started packing boxes.

My House, Your Home

So for the good reasons discussed above, we decided to set up our new home in Rock Hill in my existing house. After thinking about it for awhile, she decided she wanted to own half of my house. I told her she didn't need to spend any of her money as I was putting her on the title anyway. For some reason, she didn't feel comfortable with this, and she paid off my reverse mortgage which just happened to be half of the value we thought the house was worth. Now we own the house together, free and clear.

Moving In

As the packing progressed, I noticed that Pris was packing a lot of things we would end up with that were duplicates, broken, or excessive in one way or another. Pris always had an interesting answer when I suggested we didn't need these things. Oh, they belonged to my second husband's sister's cousin and it has sentimental value to me, or it was a gift from my first husband's mother and I couldn't possibly get rid of it, etc. We ended up packing and finally unpacking an awful lot of boxes. It's interesting that after more than three years together, she is finally starting to get rid of the excess stuff by the carload. Besides household items, she has an unusually large amount of clothes. These required using all the closets in the house, plus she had to have an additional storage unit built in the backyard to store those extras that she didn't have space for in the house and garage. Of course, you can imagine that I wasn't left with much storage space for my own things in the house.

The good news is that she sold her house right at the peak of the housing market boom of 2021 and ended up with a huge bucket of cash. She was very excited about having all the cash and ended up trying to buy everything she saw. She had previously explained that in her early years, just after college, she was forced to live very frugally with her first husband who was a small town college professor, and she was a middle school teacher in Ohio. They lived on very small incomes and didn't have many luxuries.

We now have six sets of kitchen cooking equipment, four sets of dishes and six sets of silverware. Guests come to our home for dinner and want to get a spoon or a fork, they ask which drawer to look in. We say, "which end of the kitchen are you in," because we have a full set of silverware near the stove and another full set in the eating area.

Married or Not

A subject that came up often was MARRIAGE. We discussed this occasionally, and I said that I would lose my medical insurance if we got married and I doubted that her plan would equal the cost and coverage I had under my deceased wife's plan. So we took a close look at it and there was no doubt about it. Pris's teachers plan from Ohio was far inferior to the plan I had from the California Teachers plan, which my deceased wife had obtained by working in the California school system. We decided that the costs involved were the overriding issue, and we would not tie the knot legally. I know that this is sitting in the back of Pris's mind, and some day we probably will address it again.

Last Christmas I gave her a sapphire and diamond wedding band that she hinted she wanted. She absolutely loved it, and she also loved the pledge I made to her which was a basic pledge of eternal love. I fully intend to stay with Pris for the rest of our lives.

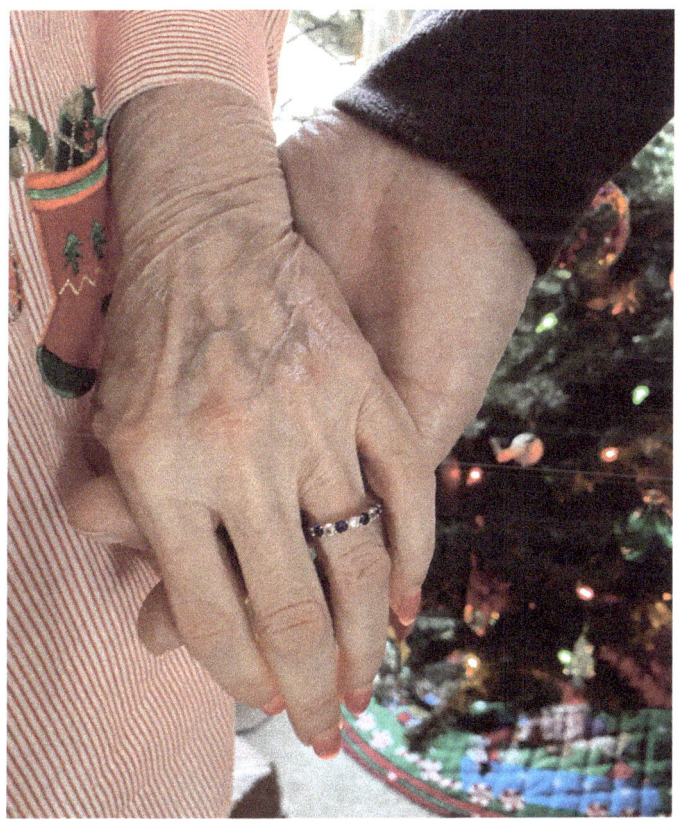

Chapter 7

EXERCISE AND HEALTH

PRIS

The year before moving to Rock Hill, I had three doctor appointments. The first two doctors said I was in perfect condition; the third doctor said that I was in good condition. I looked at the doctor and said, "No, two other doctors said that I was in perfect condition." She said that no one is in perfect condition. "I am in PERFECT condition," I replied vehemently. She laughed and said, "Okay, PERFECT condition."

Three years later in Rock Hill, I have somehow accumulated a variety of ailments. I do not blame Rock Hill or Paul for that matter. I blame "getting three years older." My first sign that my health was going to change was a trip to the emergency room. The first day was filled with tests, x-rays, etc. The second day everyone that entered my room was wearing a hazmat suit! What horrible disease did I have? All my meals changed from regular plates and silverware to paper plates and plastic silverware. After a day I asked the nurse what disease did I have that every one was wearing hazmat apparel. She looked at me and said, "I don't need this." And immediately took off her hazmat suit. To this day I do not know what disease the doctor thought I had. But it turned out to be diverticulitis which meant that I should avoid seeds and nuts to name a few foods. My sweet Paul visited me at the hospital, bringing me a little bear holding a balloon that said, "Get Well." This was a first for me. No one had ever been so thoughtful.

Later I was diagnosed as a prediabetic which caused some neuropathy in my legs. The other is acid reflux. If you are a senior and you do not have this, you are very lucky. It just means that my voice gets very raspy. These are not life-threatening ailments, for which I am thankful. We try to keep healthy by our eating habits and by exercising. I try to get 5,000 steps or more a day which, at my age, is not an easy task. When we had Piper, we would walk her around our circle twice a day. When I first met Paul we would take our first walk at 6:30 a.m.! I took care of that real fast. When I moved in, we walked her at 9:00 a.m.! Both Paul and the dog quickly acclimated themselves to this schedule. Whew!

To get more exercise in our lives, we joined the YMCA through Silver Sneakers. Silver Sneakers is a program through Medicare and insurance companies that pay for exercise programs. It is not just with YMCA because, in Pawleys Island, Paul and I joined a private physical exercise club. It is a great program for seniors; however, not all insurance companies support this program. I joined the water aerobic classes and Paul did lap swimming. He did ten laps every visit. He didn't feel that it was a lot because he told me about another swimmer in the next lane who did far more laps then he did, and he was 95!

The new rage for seniors is a sport called pickle ball. According to a friend of mine whose daughter works in the emergency room, it is also the #1 cause of injuries for seniors. In spite of these statistics, Paul and I decided to take lessons on how to play pickle ball. Paul is very competitive, but me not so much. So he quickly found me a very boring partner. I might just let his sport be pickle ball and mine golf.

Another way that I try to keep fit is playing golf. I play in a nine-hole ladies league about 30 miles away. At Pawleys Plantation where I lived previously, I only had to drive down to the clubhouse which only took two minutes. There the bag boy would go to the lockers, put my clubs on the cart, and off I would go to play golf. When I finished my golf game, the same bag boys would clean my clubs and put them away. Not so at Tega Cay, a public golf course. I had to drive 30 miles, take my clubs out of the car, and place them on the cart. When I returned, I would put the clubs from the cart into my car. No, no cleaning. I don't remember the last time my poor clubs got cleaned.

It is easy at our age to find the sofa a very comforting place to be. And the sofa certainly has a place for us older folks. But activity is a good way to keep your body in shape and, in my case, I love to hear strangers come up to me and say, "Wow, I can't believe you are 84!"

PAUL

When I first met Pris, I was a walking spare parts warehouse. I like to describe myself as a modern-day Bionic Man. I already had three orthoscopic surgeries on each knee and a knee replacement on my right knee. My right hip was replaced, and I had cataract eye surgery on both eyes. I decided to get bi-focal lens put in, so that I wouldn't need any glasses for any reason in the future. In fact the doctor told me that I didn't need cataract surgery when I had my exam. I told him I hated to wear glasses and wouldn't mind having the surgery earlier than necessary. So he did it early. I had this surgery done about 2013 and recently my eyes have started to give me trouble seeing long distances, and I am also having trouble reading. I went to the optometrist and told him what was happening, and he just told me I should get new glasses. So now I'm wearing glasses nearly all the time again. Bah! I didn't discuss any of this with Pris early on because I thought of it as ancient history and the subject never came up. She is now fully up to speed on all of my issues.

In our first year together, I had to make a trip to the hospital to have my left hip replaced. These operations are getting so routine that it hardly seems like it's something to worry about anymore. After leaving the hospital, you go home and do a few exercises, and you're as good as new. Since I had this surgery, I have been basically healthy, with no internal problems, except those I consider to be minor. I now have one new knee, two new hips and two new eyes. But there is more in the future.

About 2022, I started having bladder problems that caused me trouble controlling my urination. A trip to the doctor's office cleaned out my urethra and some pills (very expensive) keep me from running to the bathroom too often. I also have a pinched nerve in my neck that generated a lot of pain in my left arm. An injection into my neck fixed that. This left arm pain worried me because it sometimes indicates heart problems, so I was very happy to have the pinched nerve in my neck instead of a looming heart crisis.

These kinds of problems are quite new to me. I have always been very active and participated in many sports. I was active in mountain climbing, snow skiing, and soccer and I always have been very aggressive while doing them. Any trips to see the doctor or go to a hospital have always been due to some activity where I had pushed myself too hard. I always knew the reason I was getting a treatment was because of something I did and not simply because I'm getting old.

I guess I should mention that these days, it's not sports that cause me to have problems. I am a big "do-it-yourselfer," and I have had cause to see some emergency rooms over the years since we met. A brief example. I climbed a tree, not very high, but high enough to hurt myself when I fell out of it, while cutting a limb off with a chainsaw. (No, I wasn't standing on the limb that I was cutting.) The limb that I was cutting snapped off and flew back to the tree and hit me in the head, causing me to start a quick trip to the ground. So enroute to the ground, I threw the chain saw out of the way, so that I wouldn't lose any important parts from it. I solved one problem and created a new one. At this ripe old age, I was not strong enough to keep myself from free falling to the ground. All I could do was slow myself down a little while traveling downward. The trip went fine until I hit some tree burrs that ripped a good size cut in the arm I was trying to use to keep me from flying down too fast. Off to the hospital I went to get the wound cleaned up and a bunch of stitches. I hardly remember it as the damage was relatively minor.

I did take up a new sport that is more aligned with my age – Pickle Ball. We both started playing it through the Silver Sneakers program at the local YMCA. Now, this is a really fun sport that offers competition, exercise, and skill. I have grown to love the game and usually play three times a week. The crowd is generally over 60, but there are some younger players participating, which gives us older folks a really big challenge. This sport is not without its hazards. Early in learning the game, I forgot my age and tried to reach a ball that was definitely out of my reach. Well, I tried twisting to get to it and ended up crashing on my rib cage, which caused a considerable amount of pain for about three weeks. I didn't go to the doctor because they don't do much for bruised ribs. So now I play a little less enthusiastically and remember this is for fun and not the Olympic tryouts.

So what does the future hold for me? A new left shoulder. I can feel and hear the bones clicking and rubbing and the x-ray shows there is no cartilage left in the ball joint. We are going on a vacation in a few weeks, and I will have it done as soon as we come back. It's not causing any serious problems yet, and it doesn't hurt.

That's it. No known problems exist in my tired old body. My only concern is that Medicare will find some technicality to keep me from getting any work done, if it becomes necessary in the future. Right now I'm happy and enjoying my new body parts, general repairs, and no pain.

Chapter 8

HITTING THE ROAD – OUR FIRST TRIP

PRIS

I was a little on the apprehensive side when I asked Paul to accompany me to my grand-nephew's wedding outside of Denver, Colorado. To make things more complicated, this was my late first husband's family! (Did I mention that Paul was my fourth?) After all we had only been together a few months at this point. This was going to be a good test of our compatibility.

We both had a lot of airline miles so we decided to go first class. After all, at our age we should go for it! About two months after receiving our invitation to the wedding, we were UNIN-VITED! I had already made the reservations for our flight, our hotel and one week at my timeshare. The reason, it seems, that we were uninvited is that the wedding and reception venue could only accommodate 50 people because of the Covid rules. A month later we were re-invited. My daughter and son were not appreciative of being uninvited, and they decided not to attend.

We arrived in Denver with no problems but we were very disappointed with our first class accommodations. I'm sure you have noticed that, when you are in the peon's class and walk through the first class compartment, the first class passengers are sitting there enjoying their fancy drinks. Well, Covid took care of that... no drinks until after takeoff.

92

I was anxious to see my sister-in-law who would be attending the wedding. Since we were both only children, we were like sisters. But we had not seen each other for quite awhile, since we now lived so far apart. It was great to see her again. We were bussed to the wedding venue which was located outside of Denver. The wedding venue was very scenic, located on a hill overlooking a pond. The wedding was beautiful and everyone was very cordial to Paul which I very much appreciated.

Then it was off to the Colorado mountains to my timeshare. It was for a WHOLE week of 24/7 being together. It might have made us a little nervous, if it had not been for already experiencing 24/7 with Covid. If I had had any doubts about Paul, they were erased on that trip. What fun we had!

He wanted to go white water rafting which scared the bejeebies out of me. But I consented if we would go on the "family white water rafting trip" and, of course, he agreed. What I was to discover was that all white water rafting tours were the same. There was only one river available, so everyone used it – beginner to expert. The day arrived. We put on our wet suits. Paul and I were seated in the rear seat. A 10- and 12-year-old were in the middle seat. Their parents were in the front seat. Well, they are not really seats. You sit on the side of the raft and hang on for dear life! It was scary but I was really enjoying it. And then suddenly we hit a giant rapid and our guide fell off the raft! My life flashed before my eyes. My 81-year-old Paul grabbed our guide and helped him back onto the raft. The whole trip was so much fun and so delightful that whatever fears I had at the beginning were soon dissipated in the excitement of the actual trip. We filled the rest of our week with all sorts of activities, like panning for gold, enjoying the salt water spa and the scenic railroad ride.

It was on this trip I realized that I definitely hit the jackpot with Paul He was very considerate of me at all times and definitely lots of fun.

PAUL

We flew to Colorado to attend a wedding in Pris's extended family. The wedding and surrounding festivities were great fun. There was a street festival going on where we met all the relatives that Pris was close to the day before the wedding. There was lots of street food choices available. This is one of my favorite ways to eat, so I really enjoyed it. I am normally not a big drinker, but it seemed like the right thing to do with this group. So I drank somewhat, "somewhat" being a goodly amount, but not enough to embarrass myself. I was impressed by the family and how well they treated me. Remember, Pris had three husbands before me, so they have met many husbands throughout the years. I didn't sense that they felt like, "Oh God, here she is with another new guy."

That evening we went to a pre-wedding party which was pretty much a drink fest. The bar was open and the place was crowded with happy family and friends. I got into a conversation with several younger guys who were just starting out in life, and they seemed very interested in what my career was like compared to today. This got me to talk about myself, which I really love to do. I felt they were interested because of the questions they were asking me. I guess if you're young it's hard to get any input from a person with 60 years of diversified experience. I loved it.

The next day we were bussed to the wedding. It was held in a large barn-like setting in a very rural area. From our point of view, it was pretty typical (both of us had been to many weddings over the years). Once the wedding was complete, the reception was held in the same hall. There was a long period before it got going and during that time, many additional distant family members came up to Pris to say hello. They were a very diverse group. She has remained in contact with many of them throughout the years, even without seeing them very often.

We decided to tie a little vacation in with it. We went on a train ride through the mountains and were very impressed by the beautiful scenery all around us, undisturbed by cars, etc. Once again we had a challenging day on the river awaiting us. I never had noticed how many activities there are that involve water. I had always been able to swim and did lots of water activities throughout my life. Pris, on the other hand would be happy to use water for cooking and drinking only. Colorado has many white water rafting places and we felt we should do at least one. So we found one that had a beginners route and we signed up for it. I was not surprised to find out there was only one route on the river (we found that out on the river). So Pris started out very apprehensive, but she got more and more comfortable as we went along. We went a little ways before the water started to get really "white." It gave Pris a false sense of what the trip was going to be like.

About halfway through the trip, the rapids got really big. Did Pris fall out? No, the guide did. He toppled out the back. As Pris and I were sitting in the very back of the boat, we were the closest to the guide and after much effort, we pulled him back into the boat. Pris is very petite, and this was no small effort. She is getting more comfortable around water, and we may even try something more adventurous in the future.

All in all, this was a very relaxing time and we really enjoyed the week. I started to notice that once we were away from home, Pris relaxed a considerable amount and was open to try a lot of things she would not consider at home. Food was one of them. There was a Vietnamese restaurant in the hotel complex, and we tried it for lunch one day. The place was tiny and we sat at the bar to eat, which is what most folks did. WOW! the food was really good and we ended up eating there often. Cheap, good, and friendly, you can't ask for more than that. I had eaten Vietnamese food before and already knew that I would like it, if it was prepared well and it was. Pris also seemed to enjoy it because she never suggested that we go somewhere else.

Chapter 9

OUR FIRST CHRISTMAS

PRIS

I have been blessed through the years of always being with family at Christmas. The Covid virus changed many family traditions in 2020. I had just moved in with Paul. There were at least 100 boxes all over our house. I had filled my new she-shed; I had filled the cottage; I had filled my office; and the dining room had stacks of boxes as well. I think at one point I said to Paul, "I am going to my room." And he replied, "Which one?" So why was I crazy enough to offer to cook the whole Christmas dinner for my daughter and her husband? Of course, we were anxious to show off our new kitchen nook which my son-in-law had not yet seen and to entertain our first guests in OUR home.

The previous Christmas Paul had spent alone at Golden Corral, enjoying their chocolate fountain. I wondered how many people had spent this Christmas alone with no family or friends. I hope I remember that next Christmas and include someone in that situation.

Most people spend a hectic Christmas morning preparing the food and getting everything ready for the meal that would, at best, last 20 minutes. Not so for Paul and me. We shared the task. We turned to the internet to learn how to tie up a tenderloin roast and then we turned on Christmas music. Suddenly

I found myself dancing in his arms all around the kitchen. Since Paul is not the world's greatest dancer, the trip around the kitchen was not without some trips and stumbles but laughter was abundant. When I asked him to put the ironing board away, he continued the waltz with the ironing board!

Ken and Jen arrived carrying a bundle of presents to be placed under our very first Christmas tree. We decided to eat before opening presents. I must brag a little and say that the tenderloin melted in our mouths. For dessert we served frozen peppermint cake that has become my signature dessert at Christmas.

After our dinner we waddled into the living room to open our presents. Paul bought me a Bose remote speaker and a fancy charger for my phone. I was anxiously waiting for Paul to open the present that I had especially made for him. He was truly surprised and very appreciative when he opened the gift… a hand towel embroidered with: 3 P's… Pris, Paul, Piper. Later he told me that it was the best gift he had received in a long time and was very moved.

The meal had been eaten, the presents opened, and the guests departed, and now we found ourselves amidst a mountain of dirty dishes, pots and pans. But as usual, we teamed up and had the dishwasher started and the kitchen spotless in no time. I have to explain to you, however, that Paul is not a sports fan which means that he does not have to be glued to the TV on holidays. What really hit home with me is that, throughout the whole day, you could hear Paul say, "This is so great" or "This is so much fun," over and over again.

What better way to end a perfect day than to watch a heart-warming movie based on Jack London's short story, "Call of the Wild," with Harrison Ford. There we were, snuggled on the couch... not alone at Christmas.

99

Chapter 10

CONTINUING OUR ADVENTURES

PRIS

Paul had had an RV and traveled across the USA twice. I had never had the experience of traveling in an RV. Years ago I went camping with a tent. But now, at my age, that would be out of the question. However, traveling in an RV sounded like fun and a new experience for me. (Paul was the pro.) Paul was hesitant at first but agreed in the end. So off we went looking for an RV. We found the perfect one in Charleston, South Carolina. It was a 25 ft. Class C. I immediately outfitted it with items left over from our merged households. Having an RV is definitely a way to find out how really compatible you are with your mate. No problem for Miss Pris and Mr. Paul.

Our First RV Trip Together

Our first adventure was to St. Augustine, Florida At this point we did not tow a car. I made reservations at a nearby restaurant and called Uber. Fifty dollars and 45 minutes later, we arrived at the restaurant. I thought the restaurant was in downtown St. Augustine, but in reality it was far out on the marsh somewhere. I guess my map reading skills need some work! Whew!

On this trip we visited the usual touristy things, but the true highlight of the trip was going to Ponce De Leon's fountain of youth. For a mere dollar or two, we got to drink from this famous fountain. Paul decided he needed all the help he could get, so he proceeded to gulp down large amounts of the magic water. (It was also very hot.) We are sorry to report that neither one of us has seen any change in our appearance to indicate that we are getting any younger. Oh well, maybe it takes a long time to work.

On this first trip, we stayed at a state park. There are two things about state parks that are really important to know. First, they are very inexpensive for what you don't get. Second, they do not have a pump out at each camp site. They have a communal dump site that requires you to pack up your RV to get there. This requires putting everything away that could fall over or break, and unhooking the power and water. All of this to drive about a mile to unload your tanks. It's not so much the work as it is the inconvenience.

Our Second Trip

Our next adventure was in January to the west coast of Florida. We stayed at a campsite in Ruskin. It was my kind of place. Lots of activities, such as Mexican Train, poker, and even card making. One day our street had a party and we were invited. Everyone brought something to share to eat and then the games began. One game was putting a golf ball into a box with 3 holes. One hole was large and was worth 10 points. Another was a little smaller hole and worth 25 points. The third hole was very small and worth 50 points. My non-golfer Paul was the only one to hit the 50 hole, thus winning the big prize of $5! We also took a side trip to Tarpon Springs, known for its plentiful sponges. It was settled by the Greeks and is home to the largest Greek community in the United States. Of course, we had to taste some of the authentic Greek food. We met some very nice people at this campsite. One couple we would later go camping with on our trip to Kentucky.

Off Again for the Third Time

The next trip was on the Kentucky Bourbon Trail. What fun for Paul. I was the designated driver, so he got to drink all the little tasting sips, both his and mine. He was a lot of fun on the trip. One word of advice is that you need to make reservations for tours of the distilleries in advance. We did get to tour Makers Mark. We also got to see our fill of

other distilleries, despite having to work hard to find them. Before this began, we had decided a car was a necessity, so we had bought a tow dolly for this trip. Our friends from our previous Florida camping trip joined us. We visited the sites as well as the distilleries. One such

103

trip was to the Mammoth Caves. How impressive! The other historic place was to visit the birthplace of Abraham Lincoln. How great to live in a country where you can go from a log cabin to the White House.

Our Fourth and Last RV Trip

Our last trip in our RV was to the Eastern Coast of Florida the following January. Unless you have a boat, forget any socializing. Everyone had been at the campsite for years, so relationships were already formed. Thus, while everyone was socializing with old friends on their boats, we were alone in a very crowded campground!

We were in the stomping grounds of Humphrey Bogart where they filmed "Key Largo." We had drinks and dinner in the bar that they actually used to make the movie. It's really a fun place, with lots of Bogart memorabilia distributed around. We even got a chance to sit in the boat that was used in the making of the "African Queen." Paul studied the boat in great detail and pronounced it the actual original boat from the movie. We also got to go on a glass bottom boat, but I would not recommend it. The Florida reefs, at least in that section of the coast, are dying from pollution, so they are not so full of color and fish as you might expect. I had been on one before and, if you have been on one, you have probably seen it all.

The neatest thing that we did on this trip was to go to Key West. We rented a room in a darling little yellow house right downtown. We could walk everywhere. I have never seen so many roosters in my life. They were on the sidewalks, bunched in trees and even in restaurants. Roosters are protected for some reason which I forgot. One is not allowed to harm any rooster in Key West. The crowing in the morning was deafening. We visited the Truman House while we were there. I have also been to the first Truman House in Independence, Missouri. All in all, I think I prefer the West side of Florida to the East side of Florida

Our traveling in an RV is probably quite different from how most people travel. Being in our 80s, we wanted to make our trip easy and relaxing. We would travel for two hours, find a roadside park, and stop. Paul would walk Piper, and I would fix lunch. Then we would both take a short nap, get up and travel another two-three hours to our destination for the night. We would always arrange to stay a minimum of two days, in order to rest up from our trip the day before. Today, three years later, we have sold our RV but our many treasured memories will last forever.

Celebrating My 84th Birthday

I knew that Paul loved sailing. I found out that my time share provider had catamaran cruises available to trade. What a great way to celebrate my 84th birthday! When my daughter discovered that I was going on a catamaran cruise around St. Maarten, she went crazy. "Mom, you can't do that at your age. It is too dangerous." I must admit I was a little apprehensive myself, not really being a water person, and especially since I really do not know how to swim. I knew that there were catamaran cruises in Charleston. I booked a two-hour cruise around the Charleston harbor to see how I would handle being on a smaller version of what we would be doing in St. Maarten. There was not much wind on the day of our test cruise, so quite frankly it was almost boring. But at least I had had the experience and was ready to take on St. Maarten.

The other thing that I did to prepare for the trip was to take swimming lessons at the YMCA. I eventually could not only swim from one end to the other of the pool, I could also snorkel from one end to the other. However, I was to discover that the Caribbean had no walls as a safety net.

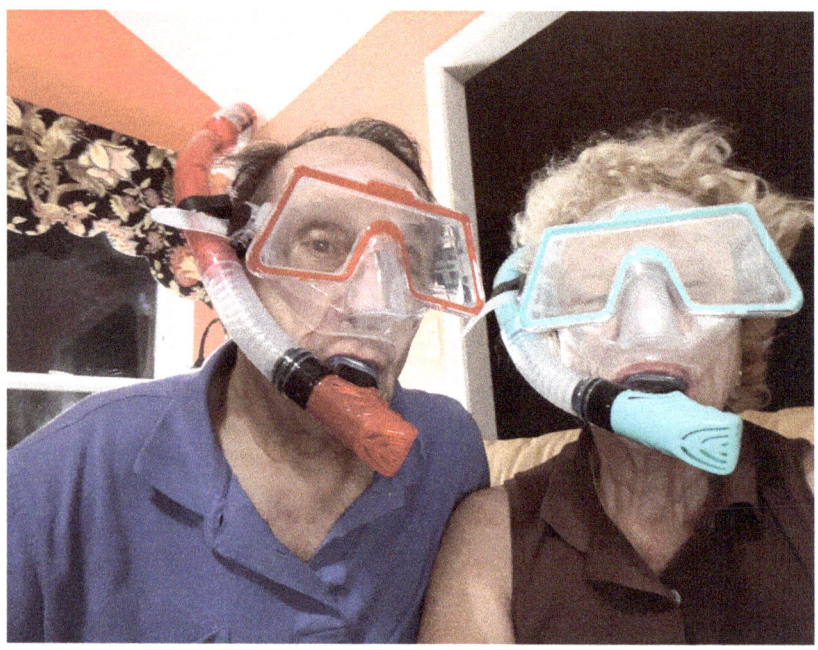

This is where getting old can be a problem. I accidentally booked our flight a day before our cruise and a day before our cruise was to end. Thus, we had to book a hotel for the first night. It turned out that this gave us a day to look around St. Maarten. Our hotel was on the Dutch side of the island. It happened to be the day of the World Cup. The United States was playing the Netherlands. We chose an open air restaurant for lunch. There was a very large screen TV in the outdoor dining area. And you guessed it. The match between the USA and the Netherlands was being played. When Paul and I cheered when

USA made a goal, all eyes in the restaurant turned to glare at us. We were the only Americans in the restaurant. Of course, the Norwegians won so the people in the restaurant became much more friendly.

The next day we boarded the catamaran with three other couples. One of my fears was that the other occupants on the catamaran would be teeny-boppers who would go topless or even worse, wear nothing at all. I was very relieved when we finally met our shipmates They were (as my daughter would say) age appropriate. Two of the couples were celebrating their 50th wedding anniversary. The other couple was younger but fit in well with the rest of us old fogeys.

We mostly motored around the island instead of actually sailing. The captain and first mate were delightful. The first mate made not only fantastic meals and hors d'oeuvres but the presentations were extra special. One time in the middle of the platter she had placed a carrot standing up in the middle of the plate with green leaves on the top to look like a palm tree. My birthday was celebrated in great style on the catamaran. A large banner displaying "Happy Birthday" was strung across the dining area. I even had a cake with candles but fortunately, not 84.

One night we took the dingy (small boat for ship-to-shore travel) to the French side of the island. Paul took me to a really fancy French restaurant to celebrate my birthday. We had about five different staff members to wait on us, one for each course. Our finale was a baked Alaska which, of course, was served to us aflame.

I know that I did not really talk about the swimming and snorkeling on the catamaran. That's because I did not do either! I did give it the "old college try" as we used to say. There was a

rope with floaters so that you could grab onto it if you needed to. That was not enough for me, however. Remember that I am a confirmed non-water person. Paul decided that maybe I could snorkel if I walked out into the water from the beach. So he swam to a nearby beach to determine how far out the beach extended into the water. It was not a difficult swim. However, when he got there a big wave came into the beach and washed his flipper into the sea. A couple sunbathing nearby saw what happened and the Frenchman jumped into the water and retrieved Paul's flipper. Paul examined the beach and discovered that there were only a few inches of sand and then a drop off. So that would not work for me. As Paul started to swim back large swells appeared and the current became strong. We all stood on the back of the catamaran, cheering him on in his difficult swim back to the boat.

All in all, the catamaran trip was mostly relaxing but also a little boring, especially because of my lack of interest in water sports. It was nice but I would not do it again.

PAUL
It's RV Time

When we got home from Colorado, Pris announced that she was ready for more travel and thought we should buy an RV. I had several over the years and had been all over the U.S. in them. I also didn't have the money to buy one and wasn't much interested in traveling anymore anyway. I expected that my couch was going to miss me.

Pris had just sold her home and had a large sum of cash burning a hole in her pocket (an old Brooklyn expression). I resisted but she spent her evenings looking on the internet and found a few she wanted to look at. So off we went to look. As I expected, she found one she liked and she bought it. She didn't want me to worry about the cost as it would be hers and paid for solely by her.

We would share driving and I would maintain it. Well, it is almost three years later and she has not driven it yet. The reason we got the size we did was so that Pris would be comfortable driving it. (HA HA) We did go to a giant school parking lot where she commenced to drive and attempt to park it, but that was the only time she got behind the wheel. I didn't mind, because RV's are quite comfortable to drive, and you don't arrive as tired as you do in a car or truck.

Each winter we picked a different area to go to. We stayed at Saint Augustine, the Tampa area, and the Florida Keys during subsequent Januaries.

We had fun traveling in it. It was very comfortable and we enjoyed the places we had been and the people we had met. This is a great way to see the country, but probably more expensive than hotel and motels. The good thing is it has a full kitchen, so eating can be cheaper than going to restaurants all the time, and there are no suitcases to lug around.

The Bourbon Trail

We also took the RV to the Bourbon Trail in Kentucky. This was a vacation planned by Pris as I had never heard of it. It was kind of exciting because to get there you must go over the Blue Ridge mountains. We were pulling my Camry behind the camper and it was a definite test of the RV's capabilities. There were lots of steep hills to go up and down. Grades as steep as 9 degrees. On the way to the Bourbon Trail, we stopped and looked at a few historic sites. We stopped at where Abe Lincoln's family started out. There are old log cabins and memorials scattered around the area. They are always a good place to stop and rest.

We stayed in some very nice campgrounds en route. We did our first tasting before we even arrived at the campgrounds in Kentucky. We never had any trouble picking distilleries. The sampling of Bourbon was quite good and because Pris doesn't drink much, she always took a little sip and gave the rest to me. I was all warm and fuzzy upon our first night's arrival. What we found the next day was that you must make reservations many months in advance to get into most tastings. We spent a large part of our day looking for places that had some extra spaces on their tours. We were not disappointed though, and we enjoyed the trip a great deal. I now have a new respect for Bourbon and it has become my drink of choice.

On the way home, there was a moonshine distillery right at the border of Tennessee and North Carolina. We stopped and had a tasting and a little history on the development of Moon Shine. Of course I had to buy a bottle. That was about a year ago, and I still have not consumed that bottle. It defi-

nitely was not as good as the Big Brands. I'm sure it will be used after all the major brands I purchased on the "Trail" are consumed.

So after three winters in Florida sunshine during the worst of the winter in South Carolina, and a trip to Kentucky, Pris decided she experienced enough of RV life and sold it. She was ready for a new car. I was just getting used to the RV life again and would have been happy to keep it.

Pris Wants To Go on a Sailboat Trip

One day while Pris was scanning through her timeshare website, she noticed that there was a sailing trip offered out of St. Maarten island, a part of the Windward Islands chain. We looked further and saw that the trip was only $2500 for both of us for an eight-day, all-inclusive vacation on a 35-foot catamaran. It had six cabins available. Pris heard me talk about my extended sailing trip many times and thought I might like a mini version to remind me of it. After all, I hadn't done much sailing in about 30 years. I jumped at the idea and felt that this was pretty inexpensive. Most trips like this cost $9-$10,000. We didn't even have to pay for the flight. We would use our air miles.

Test Drive a Catamaran

To make sure she would be comfortable on a sailboat, we went to Charleston and found a place were we could go out on a small catamaran for an afternoon. So we signed up and tested the water. She had no problems. She thoroughly enjoyed the day, and we decided to go for the Caribbean trip. Pris always likes to worry in advance and, of course, she found something to worry about for the upcoming trip – what if the girls in the other cabins are 20-year-old sex bombs going topless all the time. She said she would be afraid to show herself in a bathing suit. I put her mind at ease by reminding her that, if that were true, no one would be looking at her anyway. So off we went in early December.

Arriving at St. Maarten

We arrived in St. Maarten the day before boarding the boat and found ourselves in tourist heaven! Lots to do and see and plenty of restaurants to choose from. The local people were super friendly and couldn't wait to help with anything we might need. The next morning we went to the boat dock and found that the cleanup crew hadn't finished cleaning up our yacht yet. The taxi driver said the other guests also arrived early and went to a pub a short walk up the street. We walked into the pub and found them all having a good morning drink. We joined them and found out where they were from, etc. On our walk to the pub, we passed a marine supply store. Pris decided she needed an extra life preserver for the trip, so we went in and shopped around and she bought one for herself. I should point out that she was a little anxious about the boat part of the trip, so now that she had an extra life vest, she was starting to relax.

It was now time to board the boat. After we got our gear stowed away, we went up on deck and socialized with the other guests and met the captain and crew/cook. There was one couple on board that had made a bunch of cruises with this same company in different parts of the world. They looked much older than us and out of shape, very fat. Then there were two couples that came together, one having done multiple trips themselves. These folks were in their mid-50s or so. And us. The captain was in his 30s and the crew/cook was about 20. The captain had been with the company for quite awhile, but the cook had only sailed a few times previously with this company. They were very happy and cheery and opened the bar and served hors d'oeuvres immediately. We were introduced to the open bar policy of the boat. They had everything you could want to drink, both hard liquor and wine. It was a great start. The welcome party lasted quite a long time with lots of chatting. After a while the captain informed us that we would leave the dock and go out into the bay. We would have dinner and then spend the night at anchor. We would get underway in the morning with the tide.

The young girl who did all the cooking did an amazing job in such a small kitchen (galley). She made delicious meals that were presented as though we were on a giant cruise ship. So far, very good.

For the next several days, we island hopped over a prearranged route. We put the sails up a few times, but there was never enough wind for a good sail, or else the wind was going in the wrong direction for where we wanted to go. When we would arrive at a new island, the captain would put out a long line off the stern and hang swimming noodles on it. Then everyone would put on their life vests and jump in the water, including Pris. The swim ladder made getting on and off the boat quite easy. Some of us put on snorkel gear and left the immediate boat area to look for reefs and wild life. There was never much to see.

The places we stopped generally were isolated bays away from the frenzy of the towns, but we did stop a few times on islands with an active night life. So we did eat on shore once or twice. I think we were on the back side of St. Maarten because it was definitely a French island on which we were all going ashore for dinner. We all went our separate ways after getting ashore. There were many, many places to choose from. We had planned on one extravagant meal on the trip, so we looked for and found an upscale French restaurant with outside seating. We chose it and had an absolutely delicious meal, with superior service, including a birthday cake with sparklers on top. Pris's birthday was very soon; she was turning 84.

Back on the boat, we had celebrated Pris's birthday and a wedding anniversary on different days. The crew decorated the dining area for each occasion, and served an extra special meal.

The boat trip was really fun, even without the sailing. We got to go in the water in the middle of the winter and lounge around on deck. We spent a lot of time relaxing and reading in a foreign country, and got away from our routine life at home.

If this sounds like all we do is travel, it isn't so. Most of the things we did were not overly expensive and spread over three years, but satisfied Pris's desire to travel. Remember, we are retired. Pris had spent most of the years before she met me nursing a very sick husband. She didn't get out very much during that time. I am more of a homebody and would be just as happy

staying in Rock Hill. But Pris really likes to travel, and it was hard to say no to the trips she wanted to go on.

As the time passed in our relationship, we grew together whether we were at home or on a trip somewhere. Money is generally not a big concern as we both are able to support ourselves comfortably. The problems of married life for younger folks is they have so many to deal with, like jobs, kids, money, etc., that distract them from focusing on each other. For us, it's only each other and medical problems. Neither one of us has any serious medical problems, so we have a very simple life, relatively speaking.

Chapter 11
STILL SMILING AFTER THREE YEARS

PRIS

Three years have passed. Did I make the right decisions? Did I make the right decision to sell my house at the beach and leave all of my friends? I loved my house at Pawleys Island, but it was just a house. To be a home, it needs love and someone to share it with. When I moved in with Paul, I found all of that and a whole lot more, beyond my wildest dreams.

Finding a Church

Of course I miss my friends and all of the activities I was involved in… my church, book club, golf, scrapbooking, investment club, and bridge. But this was during the pandemic, so I do not know how many of these activities I could have enjoyed if I had stayed in Pawleys Island. So only knowing Paul in Rock Hill, I had to search for activities that I could enjoy. The first search was to find a church. Being a Presbyterian in Pawleys, I looked into Presbyterian churches near me. There was one just around the corner but it turned out to be too fundamental for me. I ended up joining the First Presbyterian Church in downtown Rock Hill. Paul and I joined a dine-around group sponsored by the church. This way we get to know people more intimately.

Newcomer's

The next thing I did was to see if there was a Newcomer's Club. I found that there was a York County Newcomer's Club, called their phone number, and made my first friend in Rock Hill. The Newcomer's Club has all sorts of activities including bridge, book clubs, and socializers. These are the ones I joined, but there were many more to choose from. I am now on the board as the club Historian – working on the scrapbook is right up my alley. One of the other activities is Socializers. Paul and I signed up to have one of these at our house. We had 25 people attend. Everyone brought a food or wine to share. We had croquet, badminton, corn hole, a putting green, and yard Yahtzee available for our guests to enjoy. Paul and I really enjoyed planning for and entertaining our guests.

Golf

My new friend invited me to join a non-newcomers group, the 9-hole golfers at Tega Cay. I was not only used to storing my clubs at the club house in Pawleys, I was used to having the bag boys put them on the cart and clean the clubs when I was finished. Not here... a public course. So, not only did I have to take my own clubs out of the car but also had to put them on the cart. Since I had to clean them as well, it is safe to say the clubs did not get cleaned often. The 9-holers are a fun group and at 84, I am still playing and loving it.

My New Neighborhood

The most disappointing thing about my choice was the neighborhood. I had lived in a sharing and loving community where everyone was there for each other. Not here! Since we could not participate in outside events during Covid, Paul and I walked the dog twice a day. We did meet some people walking. There was one couple we stopped and talked with quite often as we walked. So when the Covid had slowed down and people were getting together again, we invited them to dinner. Their response was that they really did not like socializing. So what I have learned is that people who live on an acre, live on an acre because they do not want to socialize. Also, my one neighbor is very unfriendly so I stay away from them. This makes me very sad because I believe in the Bible which says, "Love your neighbor as yourself." I will say that now after three years we have become friends with the new neighbor across the street, even though they are my grandchildren's age. They still seem to enjoy our company, I think! We do socialize with the neighbor on the other side of us and they are very friendly. They have recently decided to raise chickens; thus, we are never without eggs.

Quality Time With My Daughter

A great positive about moving to Rock Hill is that I get to see my daughter often. She was president of the Women's Auxiliary of the Salvation Army of Greater Charlotte. I joined them also to support her, something that I never would have had the opportunity to do if I had not moved to Rock Hill. She makes time to come visit me regularly. Paul and I enjoy going up to their home on Lake Norman and spending some time with them on their boat or enjoying one of my daughter's delicious meals. She and her husband bought a pizza oven, so now we get to enjoy her delicious homemade pizzas.

Piper

Another positive in my new life was Piper. My Cody having died just before Paul and I met, I was happy to have another dog. Recently, because she is 17 and ailing, we thought we might have to put her down. We took her to a different vet to get another opinion about what to do. She had arthritis in her back legs and had difficulty standing up and going up and down stairs. The new vet said that Piper was lucky to have such caring parents and that other than her arthritis she was in great condition for her age. She gave her a shot that seemed to have helped her to cope better with the arthritis. Two weeks later, we had to put her down. Paul dug her a grave in the woods behind our house and put up a cross on which he hung her dog collar and tags. We can see it from our kitchen nook. This was a very tough time for both of us, being unable to help our little Piper as she tried to maneuver around the house. It made me feel like crying. Losing a dog like her is like losing a member of the family. We both miss her and think about her often.

Crafting

For the past 20 years I had been a Creative Memories consultant. Creative Memories is an online scrapbooking business. I loved making scrapbooks for myself, but I sometimes would make scrapbooks for friends and family, if we had taken a trip together or for a special occasion. I made more than 30 books for one lady of her three children. I also had a large group of people who would come to my classes at my house. We sometimes would go on retreats. One time one of the ladies had a large house on the beach that would accommodate all of us. What a blast that was! It was a ladies all-night slumber party!

The ladies still meet today 20 years later twice a month just to make cards and chat.

When I moved to Rock Hill, it was during Covid so I had to put my scrapbooking and card making aside. But once Covid had lessened, I started making cards again. I found some churches that were having craft fairs so I entered them. I am having fun participating in the fairs but I certainly won't get rich!

I also had some of the ladies from my new neighborhood over several times to show my cards at Christmas time. This was a great way to make some new friends in the neighborhood, and we have since become very good friends.

The really neat thing that happened was that I found some ladies from Stampin'up (another online craft business) who also loved to make cards. So we meet quarterly at each other's houses and then once a year we go on a three-day retreat.

Now about Paul

Did I make a mistake making him my lifelong partner? Absolutely not! Yes, probably the initial excitement has toned down slightly, but we still make sure to give each other a good-night and good morning kiss. Besides the "options" episode, we've had very few unpleasant moments. Paul had been living alone for eight years, so he had developed habits about the way he did things. One little problem we had was that I did not do things exactly the way he did. I have to say that some of them were legitimate complaints, like not turning off the oven light when I was finished baking or not screwing the lid on tight on almost every jar in the house. These things drove Paul crazy. So finally, I approached Paul and asked him to please not point out to me every little thing I did wrong. I asked him just to do it and go on about his day. He immediately made every effort to do this. And I have to say he has done an excellent job. He often says to me, "Isn't this great," as we are finishing up one of our many delicious meals, or when we are just sitting together on the porch. We both love to cook and have so much fun thinking up new ideas of what to make next.

One thing we do is something that just happened one day. We both hate emptying the dishwasher. So we decided that he would put away the silverware and I would do the rest. Then one day we bet a "dishwasher" on something ,and we have been doing it ever since. We bet on simple things, like who the murderer is in a movie, or where we ate dinner last week (old folks have bad memories). What that means is whoever loses the bet has to empty the whole dishwasher by themselves. It's like a game and we always laugh about the competition that comes from it.

To sum it all up…YES!!! It is definitely one of the best decisions I ever made. Paul and I are happy to have each other, and we demonstrate daily our love for each other. I thank God every day for giving me Paul as my partner and for giving us our relatively good health, both at 84.

PAUL

As I think back over the past three years, it is obvious that we both are very aware of our ages and know that we probably don't need a ten-year plan for our future. We are very grateful that we found each other and try to keep in mind that there aren't many people as lucky as we are. Sometimes she frustrates me and other times she makes me marvel at her personality, wit, and intelligence. She has a black thumb around computers and she will not ride an escalator, go above the second step of a ladder, and wears several life jackets when near the water. But this is Pris and I love her for it.

When I first met Pris, she told a few jokes occasionally. Now that we are really comfortable with each other, she is basically a laugh a minute and keeps me laughing hysterically. I am impatient and nag her about some of the ways she cooks, but her meals are always delicious. On the other hand she is the world's biggest back seat driver. She not only watches my speed, she tells me to watch this or that about other drivers. She gives me directions even when we are using the GPS. She absolutely cannot refrain from doing these things.

She also will bend over backwards to help me with a project, anticipate my needs or desires, and is always ready to compliment my work or knowledge. She will do things for me, like prepare a snack, iron a shirt, find my glasses, or prepare drinks (we have to get rid of all the booze we bought on the Bourbon

Trail). I wouldn't change a thing, because all of it adds up to the one and only genuine Pris.

A common expression is that you're not marrying just the woman, but the whole family. Well, I knew this to be true and didn't know what to expect. I have to say that not only do I get along with Pris's daughter but also feel that I have an excellent relationship with her husband Ken. But there's more. The grandkids are also great and I really like them. Family gatherings are nothing less than pleasant and I love to go to their home. We even have a vacation planned with Ken and Jen in the near future. I know it will be a special memory at its conclusion. So not only did I get a great partner, I got a whole great family thrown in. What a bargain!

My problem, that I'm sure Pris will point out, is my impatience with things done less than the most efficient, easiest way possible. I expect her to have the same knowledge using computers as I have, which accumulated over 40 years of intense computer usage. Teachers didn't use them very much when she was teaching. In any case, these are things for both of us to watch. I try really hard to keep my mouth shut, and I'm sure she does the same. Hugs fix a lot of things.

We often talk about death and dying because we are so close to experiencing this last great adventure. Neither one of us wants a viewing or funeral. We agree that both of us will be cremated. I want my ashes to go into the ocean, but Pris does not seem to care what happens to hers. I'm sure her daughter will probably want them. We don't want to be kept alive if we are at or near vegetables and don't want to wait around for a cure if there isn't one available at the moment for the bug we might end up with.

Neither of us wants to go to an old folks home. We want to die at home and we have made a solemn commitment that we will take care of each other for as long as is possible. In my view this does not seem to be a large problem. If Pris has some ailment that keeps her from taking care of herself, then my only reason for being alive at that point will be to take care of her. I don't think it will be a burden. But that appears to be a long ways away. We both are still pretty healthy and happy. We are always making more plans for the future.

When compared to our friends, we appear to be in above-average condition, with some aches and pains that seem to be controllable with over-the-counter drugs.

My mind is pretty sharp, although not everybody would agree with that statement. When I play poker, I do well in the early stages of the game. But as the evening wears on, my memory and logic skills deteriorate rapidly, so I am usually home early (get knocked out of the game – go home). I did finish third and won a sizable cash prize in the WSOP Seniors tournament (55 and over) last year at the Cherokee Casino in North Carolina. Pris thinks I can do it again, so she doesn't mind my going there alone to try my luck whenever there is a major event.

The bottom line is that before I met Pris,

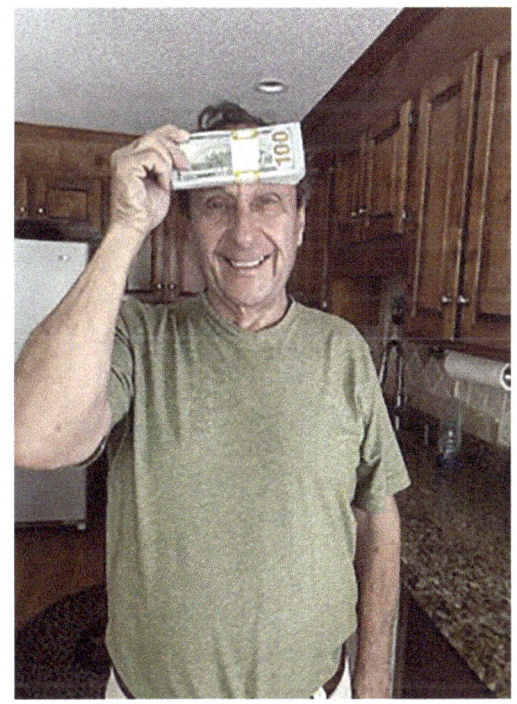

my life was basically a pile of misery. I wasn't happy, had no hope of being happy, and couldn't see anything positive in my future. Now I am happy nearly all the time, couldn't imagine life without her. We wake up with at least a kiss every morning, and go to bed the same way. If we are sitting in the living room, we are always snuggled up together on the couch.

After proofreading this book, I notice that as we describe something we did together, the section always ends with how hard we laughed at the conclusion of our various activities, or how much fun we had. That's a lot of smiling, laughing and good cheer.

So what more can I now say about my day-to-day life:
"Isn't Life Grand?!"

FAVORITE RECIPES

A couple from Pris:
No Sugar Apple Pie (This recipe won Best Dessert of the Year in the Cleveland Plain Dealer)

1 6 oz can frozen apple juice concentrate
1 Tbsp margarine
2 Tbsp cornstarch
1 tsp cinnamon
1/4 tsp nutmeg
6 cups peeled sliced Delicious apples
pastry for 2-crust pie

Place apple juice concentrate in saucepan; bring to a boil. Combine margarine, cornstarch and spices in small bowl. Add a small amount of apple juice; stir until well blended. Stir cornstarch mixture into apple juice. Pour over apples; stir carefully to coat all slices. Pour into unbaked pie crust; place top crust over apples. Bake at 425 degrees for about 30 minutes. Reduce temperature to 375 degrees; bake for 30 minutes longer.

Thanks to:
Hilda Wright
Huntsville, Alabama

Old Fashioned Sweet-Sour Cole Slaw
(This recipe is from the restaurant at Brookville Hotel now located in Abilene, KS. It was originally in Brookville, Kansas, built in 1870. It is famous because it is rumored that Wild Bill Hickock stayed there.)

1-1/2 lb shredded green cabbage
1 tsp salt
2/3 cup sugar
1/3 cup cider vinegar
1 cup whipping cream (do not whip)

Place shredded cabbage in covered dish in the refrigerator for several hours. Mix ingredients in order given 30 minutes before serving. Add to cabbage. Chill and serve.

Clam Chowder the Easy Way (This won 2nd at our church soup contest)

1 pkg. potato soup mix
1 can whole clams

Follow instructions on the potato soup package. When cooked, add the clams and the juice (important to add the juice because it adds flavor).
Serve and enjoy.

And now – one from Paul:

Noodles and Cheese
This is a dish I make very often and is very easy, quick, and surprisingly delicious. We have it when we want something real quick without a lot of work. This was one of my staples as I went through college.

It has just 4 ingredients - Serves 6
1 pkg of wide egg noodles
1 cube of butter
1 large white onion – chopped   (I sometimes use two onions – it can't hurt)
1 large pkg of large curd cottage cheese – removed from the refrigerator, to let come to room temperature.

Take a little of the butter, melt in a frying pan, add the onion and sauté over a low to medium flame, until golden brown.
While the onion is cooking, boil the noodles per the instructions on the pkg.
If you follow this order, the onions and the noodles should be done at about the same time
Place the rest of the butter in the pot with the onions (you may want to chop the butter a little so it melts faster)

Drain the noodles thoroughly
Mix in the buttered onions
Mix in the cottage cheese
Enjoy
(this recipe can be frozen)

Pris Keefer graduated from Bethany College in 1961. She obtained her Master's Degree in Supervision from Baldwin-Wallace College. She taught middle school in the Berea City School System teaching Spanish, English and American history where she was honored as Teacher of the Year. She was on the board and served as president of the Juvenile Diabetes Foundation of Greater Cleveland. She retired in 1996 to South Carolina where she taught GED and English as a second language at Horry-Georgetown College in Myrtle Beach, S.C. She and Paul met in 2020 when both were in their 80s. This is her first work as a writer which describes their love story at the age of 81.

Paul Mikos was born in Brooklyn, N.Y. in March 19, 1939. He joined the 101st Airborne Div as a paratrooper when he was 19. He went to Northrop University and received a degree in Electronic Engineering after leaving the service. He worked as a circuit designer and software developer in the aerospace industry for several years. He then went on his own for the next five years doing consulting in the same field. He eventually left aerospace to work in sales technical support and then sales for a startup mini-computer company. After a few years he went on his own to develop business software programs for small to medium-size companies.

Eventually he left technical work entirely and became an entrepreneur to start several technical companies in California's Silicon Valley. He retired at the age of 50 to take a three-year sailing cruise through the western hemisphere. Pricilla is Paul's second wife. He has two children. This book is Paul's first attempt at authorship.

130

Praise for *Finding Love at 80*

"I finished your book. I absolutely love it! What a beautiful love you have! I hope tons of single seniors read it and get hope for their futures! Kudos – well done!"

—Michele M.

"Have finished your book. What an easy read!!! How fortunate for Paul and you to meet each other. I believe you are so compatible/incompatible at the same time. Keeps life interesting!! Here's to many more years together."

—Mary Lou L.

"Adults of all ages can enjoy this uplifting story shared by two extraordinary octogenarians. For all of us already labeled as 'seniors' in this world, this story can truly inspire us to live every day trying to improve our attitudes toward aging and looking forward to the future. It exudes the power of positivity in our lives at all ages. As shown in this story, age does not limit our desire and want to love and be loved. Younger adults may not be aware of the needs and thoughts of seniors... this subject is rarely discussed by writers, addressed in movies or television, or even discussed among friends. Hopefully, many will be enlightened by what they read in this book. The writers are truly an amazing couple, and I thank them for sharing their happy and thought-provoking story."

—Beverly H.

"Such a beautiful, endearing story of finding love at a time when you truly believed you'd be alone. These authors instill renewed hope in all of those who thought their time for sharing life with another had passed them by. It's an honest reflection of expectations, surprises, fun, and unforeseen issues that arise with a new relationship at this stage of your life. They remind us all of the importance of maintaining a sense of humor, the willingness to compromise, and most of all the ability to keep an open heart to love when it comes knocking."

—Karen R.